NATIONALISM IN THE MIDDLE AGES

NATIONALISM IN THE MIDDLE AGES

Edited by C. LEON TIPTON
Lehigh University

HOLT, RINEHART AND WINSTON
New York • Chicago • San Francisco • Atlanta
Dallas • Montreal • Toronto • London • Sydney

Cover illustration: The battle of Formigny, 1450, from *Chroniques de Charles VII* by Jean Chartier. *(Bibliothèque Nationale, Paris)*

CONTENTS

Introduction   1

THE ORIGINS OF NATIONALISM

HANS KOHN – The Modernity of Nationalism   7
JOHAN HUIZINGA – Nationalism in the Middle Ages   14
MARC BLOCH – Medieval National Consciousness   25
JOSEPH R. STRAYER – Laicization and Nationalism in the
    Thirteenth Century   30
BOYD C. SHAFER – The Early Development of Nationality   40

FACTORS IN THE DEVELOPMENT OF MEDIEVAL NATIONALISM

VIVIAN H. GALBRAITH – Language and Nationality   45
FREDERICK HERTZ – War and the Formation of National
    Traditions   54
THOMAS F. TOUT – Feudal Allegiance and National Sentiment   59
ERNST H. KANTOROWICZ – Patriotic Propaganda   65
GEORGE G. COULTON – The Papacy   70
FREDERICK HERTZ – The Role of the Medieval Church   75
GAINES POST – Legal Theory   79

CASE STUDIES

BARNABY C. KEENEY – England   87
DOROTHY KIRKLAND – France   98
GIFFORD DAVIS – Castile   108

Suggested Additional Readings   115

The artist who executed the miniature in this thirteenth-century French manuscript included thirteenth-century armor and siege weapons in his portrayal of an Old Testament battle. (*The Pierpont Morgan Library*)

INTRODUCTION

In most textbooks the student of European history first discovers nationalism at about the same time that he encounters the French Revolution; thereafter he is chiefly concerned with describing, analyzing, and evaluating the new "ism." At the end of this process he is driven to the inescapable conclusions that nationalism has been one of the great historical forces of recent times and that a knowledge of its nature and influence is absolutely essential to an understanding of contemporary Europe. Regrettably, the time of its introduction, and its immediate and continuing importance, also conspire to incline him toward the idea that it is a phenomenon first appearing in—and germaine only to—the modern age. This widely accepted notion is, in itself, a "problem." That is to say, to the extent that it ignores the origins and evolutionary development of national sentiment, it disregards the continuity of history and thus misrepresents the past.

Much of our understanding of nationalism is muddled by the need to periodize history. In an attempt to impose order upon the vastness and complexity of the human past we have divided it into various chronological segments which we designate "ancient history," "medieval history," "modern history," and so on. The consequence of this necessary and valuable teaching technique is to accustom us to think of most things as falling entirely within the purview of one of these artificial epochs. For example, students often think of feudalism as something applicable only to the Middle Ages and nationalism as something pertinent only to the modern era. The truth is, of course, that facets of feudalism survived medieval times and elements of nationalism are found before the modern period. Such great historical "isms" are usually born slowly and die the same way. To grasp this fundamental point is to lay hands upon the truth of historical continuity.

The primary purpose of this book is to introduce students to the scholarly debate concerning the origins, development, and essentials of premodern nationalism. That such a debate exists and that the differences of interpretation are often fundamental should be quickly apparent after reading the first few selections. Thus one student of the subject claims that nationalism, as we understand the term today, did not exist at all in the Middle Ages. From such a conclusion another historian vigorously dissents, arguing that things need not have

1

a name and a modern definition in order to have existence. From this he goes on to say that nationalism was a viable force in the medieval world.

Although the authors of the present essays approach nationalism from various angles and reach different conclusions, most have one thing in common: they are convinced that the proper place to begin an investigation of the growth of national sentiment is the medieval period. In this connection it is important to remember that most of them qualify their remarks by enclosing the term nationalism in quotes, referring to it as "national consciousness," "incipient nationalism," "latent nationalism," and so on. This should not be interpreted as an attempt on their part to avoid taking a firm scholarly position. It is rather a simple acknowledgment of the fact that the term nationalism has no real synonym in the English language. To discuss nationalism in its infancy one must coin new terms—which historians are notoriously reluctant to do—or point out by the use of qualifying phrases that it was somewhat different in the Middle Ages from what it has been in recent times.

In the first selection Hans Kohn states the thesis commonly found in European history textbooks, namely, that there was no sentiment worthy of being called nationalism in the Middle Ages. According to him nationalism exists only when the majority of men give their first loyalty to the state, and since this situation did not prevail in the Middle Ages, nationalism was absent. The entire medieval world, the Greek and Arabic portions as well as the Latin West, had as its first principle religious unity. Moreover, these three cultures possessed a world view that placed God and the salvation of the soul above allegiance to princes and concern for the state. Within such a framework nationalism was impossible.

Kohn warns us that we should not interpret the writings and deeds of medieval men in the light of modern nationalism but rather in the context of their own time. Simply stated, we should not read the present into the past. Thus, we should avoid using the words of a medieval writer as evidence of nationalism unless we can show that his opinion represented something more than an atypical utterance. This approach, combined with his concept of what modern nationalism is, virtually closes the door to the possibility of medieval nationalism: Medieval men did not give their first allegiance to the state, and if a few did, or argued that one should, they were atypical. A basic question for the reader is, of course, whether he should accept Kohn's methods and definition.

In the next selection Johan Huizinga asks the question: Should we, in seeking the initial evidence of nationalism, be bound by modern terminology and definitions? No more basic query could be put to students of history. Do we read history forward or backward? Should we say nationalism did not exist in the Middle Ages because the word nationalism had not been coined or because no one had bothered to formulate concepts that fit our modern definition? Would Shakespeare's rose smell as sweet or be any less real if it had no name at all?

Basically, Huizinga's position is that nationalism is an emotional attitude

or state of mind and that the equivalent to our modern definition of that sentiment existed in the medieval period. It is true, he admits, that modern nationalism is more visible than the medieval variety, but he denies that it is something
completely new. In attempting to prove this point Huizinga uses evidence from
all periods and phases of the Middle Ages. Hans Kohn did the same. How can
historians ask themselves the same question, survey the same literature, men, and
events, and produce such different interpretations?

Marc Bloch, the renowned French medievalist, surveys the feudal society
of medieval Europe and concludes that language played a vital role in pro-
ducing a highly developed sense of "national consciousness" among the peoples
of Europe by the beginning of the twelfth century. The terms used by medieval
men to describe their "nation" reveal, in his opinion, a gradual movement in the
direction of nationalism. Bloch recognizes, of course, that there are obvious
differences in the attitudes and feelings of medieval and modern men toward the
concept of the *fatherland*, but he argues that the idea of a *fatherland* is, in itself,
proof of a rudimentary national feeling.

Joseph R. Strayer finds that although nationalism was not yet a "respectable
force at mid-thirteenth century," by the end of the same century men were more
and more inclined to give their primary allegiance to lay governments. "Laicization," as he calls this process, necessarily involves the gradual decline of church
power in terms of claims to univeralism and a gradual development of royal
power. By the end of the thirteenth century lawyers interested in justifying this
shift of allegiance had developed a theory not far removed from the modern concept of the sovereign state.

Concurrent with the shift of men's allegiances, monarchs began to deliberately encourage nationalism as a force useful to their ends, and Strayer cites numerous examples of such encouragement. The effect of these royal efforts was to lift
nationalism onto a new plateau and put the weight of the state behind it. Thus
nationalism contributed to the formation of nations, and the emergence of nations contributed to a heightened sense of national feeling. In this respect nationalism was both cause and effect of nation building.

In the last selection dealing with the problem of the origins of nationalism,
Boyd C. Shafer stresses the complexity and interrelationship of the many factors
that produced modern nationalism and cautions us to avoid seeking a "single
hypothesis" to explain its appearance. At the same time he warns that in studying
the Middle Ages we should not see "forces which might later develop into nationalism as the thing itself." In other words, medieval national sentiment was
the precursor of modern nationalism but the two are significantly different. Again
the reader should ask himself: How is it that Shafer, using the same evidence
as Kohn and Huizinga, manages to end up with a thesis somewhere in the middle.

The first five selections should make it clear that scholars are not agreed
upon the subject of medieval nationalism. Kohn says that it did not exist, Huizinga that it did. Strayer finds it "respectable" only at the end of the thirteenth

century; Bloch believes it was present at the beginning of the twelfth. Shafer is of the opinion that what Strayer, Huizinga, and Bloch are writing about was considerably different from what he and Kohn are discussing. It would seem that in this case our selected scholars have justified the opinion of the wag who said history was "the promotion of past confusion to the present."

The purpose of presenting these conflicting interpretations of medieval nationalism is not to promote confusion but to stimulate the reader's thinking. What is the nature of nationalism? Is it an emotion, an attitude, an idea, or a political state of affairs? If it is an emotion or attitude, how does one measure such sentiments in remote historical periods? How can a historian judge what is typical or atypical of an earlier age? These are some of the questions to bear in mind when considering the arguments and evidence contained in the second group of selections.

In this section a number of historians discuss various factors that contributed to the development of national feeling. For them the question is not "Was there nationalism in the Middle Ages?" but rather "What was the nationalism of the Middle Ages?" Note, however, that in their treatments of the subject they deal with many of the same elements of nationalism that are dealt with in the first section; namely, language, war, propaganda, and the Church.

The test most often applied to detect nationalism is that of language: it is argued that people who speak alike are inclined to think alike. Moreover, as languages are a product of historical development, it follows that those who use the same tongue have experienced the same history. Thus to have language in common is also to have the same traditions. These and related elements of nationalism are the subject of Vivian H. Galbraith's essay on medieval England.

Interestingly enough, Galbraith stresses the fact that English "nationalism" cannot be equated with the use of the vernacular alone. On the contrary, we must look to the educated men of the Middle Ages for our first signs of its appearance and that means the Latin chroniclers. As simply stated as possible, Galbraith is saying that nationalism is an attitude, a state of mind, an idea, and that these remain the same regardless of the language used in thinking or writing about them. In this connection note that the chroniclers mentioned by most of our authorities wrote in Latin.

Of all the forces that account for the rise of national sentiment, war is the most frequently underestimated. We are accustomed today to think of wars as the result of excessive nationalism; we seldom think of nationalism as the result of excessive wars. The latter point is discussed by Frederick Hertz in his brief but important essay on the development of national traditions. According to this interpretation war was a major factor in the creation of national unity in that it excited a common hatred and a common pride among the population of any country engaged in combat.

The selection from the writings of Thomas F. Tout examines the relationship between nationalism and feudalism. In Tout's view the breakdown of the latter system in the late thirteenth and early fourteenth centuries resulted in the transfer of the allegiance of the individual from the local lord to the king. In this way the decentralized and contractual feudal system with its emphasis upon loyalty to a higher lord was able to rise above localism and prepare the way for national unity and a rudimentary national feeling. But the transition was neither short nor easy. Tout is quick to point out that despite the general trend "English" barons followed Simon de Montfort, a "Frenchman," when he rebelled against an "English" monarch, and that the Burgundians sided with England and against France in the Hundred Years' War. A final point: in reading this essay one would do well to note Tout's brief remarks about the role of the Church in the creation of nationalism and to recall them when studying subsequent selections dealing specifically with this aspect of the problem.

Ernst H. Kantorowicz's essay compliments Strayer's contribution on "laicization." The latter concludes his study with the struggle between Philip the Fair and Boniface VIII and the use of nationalism made by the king in his struggle with the pope; Kantorowicz takes up the story from that point and develops Strayer's thesis in detail, referring to the king's appeal to national sentiment as simply "patriotic propaganda." Philip asked all Frenchmen to come to the aid of their country against its outside enemies. In short, the appeal was made to what is today called one's "love of country." To stand with the *fatherland* and the king in the national struggle with the papacy was to stand for justice, culture, Christianity, and all else that was good. Does this attitude seem similar to the propaganda broadsides of 1789, 1848, or 1914?

George G. Coulton finds evidence of a strong national sentiment in the desire of the French and of the Italians to elect one of their own nationality as pope. Indeed, in his judgment the history of the Church in the later Middle Ages is largely determined by national considerations. The end result of this process was, by the beginning of the modern era, a "nationalized papacy" which in turn produced a spirit of independence in France (Gallicanism) and an open rebellion against the Church in Germany. Basically Coulton agrees with the preceding comments of Tout on the role played by the Church in the creation of nationalism; he differs in that he places emphasis upon the institution of the papacy rather than upon the ecclesiastical structure in its entirety.

The next essay in this section is somewhat broader in its approach. Here Frederick Hertz argues that by taking the lead in reducing the loose tribalism of the early Germans to "wider and firmer regional communities" the Church encouraged a political process that was to culminate in the European state system. As this gradual consolidation took place, the frequent struggles between popes and secular rulers forced people to choose between the national state and the international church, a choice that was increasingly resolved in favor of the former.

While Hertz does not clearly say so, he implies that the Church was really the innocent victim of the nationalism it had helped to create.

In the last selection in this group Gaines Post studies the relationship of legal theory to the development of nationalism. In the course of this he shows how the legal offensive mounted by Vicentius Hispanus, a Spanish legist, against the claims of sovereignty by the Holy Roman Emperor were foreshadowings of the decline of universalism and the rise of national loyalties. In the end he makes it clear that the nationalistic direction in which Europe was moving was not only the work of popes, kings, and knights, but of lawyers as well.

In the final section of the book examples of medieval nationalism in England, France, and Castile are examined by three historians: Barnaby C. Keeney, Dorothy Kirkland, and Gifford Davis. Their essays require little comment, as in each case the arguments rest largely upon one or more of the broader "factors" discussed in the preceding section. When reading each example, however, one should correlate the evidence given with the general thesis of each of the scholars who wrote on the problem of the origins and elements of medieval nationalism.

The cumulative effect of the scholarship presented here should raise major historical questions in the reader's mind. What were the origins of nationalism? When and why did it appear in Europe? Can we date its beginnings with any precision? Where are the examples of its existence in the Middle Ages? And, finally, what are the similarities and differences between medieval nationalism and the nationalism we have seen in modern times? Such questions as these do not, of course, lend themselves to "scientific" or definitive answers; the most one can hope for is a sound and reasonable interpretation based on solid historical evidence. If such an interpretation suggests itself to the reader, the present essays will have contributed something toward an understanding of the problem of nationalism in the Middle Ages.

In the reprinted selections footnotes appearing in the original sources have in general been omitted unless they contribute to the argument or better understanding of the selection.

The Czech-born scholar HANS KOHN (1891–1971), late professor of European history at The City College of New York, maintains that nationalism is a product of the modern era. In his view the major institutions of the medieval world, the universal church and feudalism, rendered impossible any sentiment worthy of being called nationalism. His thesis concerning the modernity of nationalism has been extremely influential in shaping the ideas of modern European historians, and it would not be unfair to say that his conclusions represent the majority opinion of that group.*

Hans Kohn

The Modernity of Nationalism

In the Middle Ages, the period of the Western Roman Empire created by the Pope, nationalism, in the sense understood today, did not form any essential part of the communal mind. Of course, there was a primitive and natural feeling of community of language or homeland, especially in the latter part of the Middle Ages, and of tribal cohesion in the earlier part. But the decentralization and differentiation within those bodies which were later to form the future nations in no way allowed the growth of that political and emotional integration which is the basis of modern nationalism. Economic life was confined to the practically self-sufficient large estates and cities. No uniform law or jurisdiction encour-

aged the development of a common feeling of nationality.

The whole intellectual and emotional life of man and the political and social ideal of organization were dominated by religious concepts and norms; in a way scarcely imaginable to us, they colored and determined the thought and feeling of every minute of life, at work and at play, in public and in solitude, in every grief and every joy, in fear and hope, for the artist and for the tiller of the soil. This religion was universal. Its dominance left no room for any decisive influences of nationalism. Practically all learning and writing were in the hands of the clerics who used one common language, Latin. People looked upon everything

* Reprinted with permission of The Macmillan Company from *The Idea of Nationalism: A Study of Its Origins and Background* by Hans Kohn, pp. 78–85, 93–96. Copyright 1944 by Hans Kohn. Footnotes omitted.

not from the point of view of their "nationality" or "race," but from the point of view of religion. Mankind was divided not into Germans and French and Slavs and Italians, but into Christians and Infidels, and within Christianity into faithful sons of the Church and heretics.

Towards the end of the Middle Ages national states began to take shape, and the first foundations for the future growth of nationalism were laid. A few individuals wrote and acted in a way which would justify claiming them for nationalism. But they were isolated individuals, extremely interesting as forerunners, but without any immediate influence upon their people and their time. It would be misleading to interpret sayings and deeds of the later Middle Ages or of early modern times in the light of modern nationalism, instead of trying to understand them under their own conditions. Some of the examples adduced to prove the existence of nationalism in the later Middle Ages, if seen in their context, allow an entirely different interpretation. Pertinent and interesting utterances in the sources may have been preserved for the very reason that they expressed attitudes unusual for that time.

The political thought of the Middle Ages was characterized by the conviction that mankind was one and had to form one community. The new Roman Empire was instituted as an instrument of religious universalism. Its task was "ad fidem in gentibus propagandam, prout ad predictionem evangeli sacrum Romanum imperium preparavit" ["To propagate faith in the nations just as the Holy Roman Empire prepared them for the preaching of the gospel"—Ed.]. Since Christendom in the Middle Ages was coextensive with humanity, at least as a goal, mankind was regarded as one people, a *res publica generis humani* ["com-

monwealth of the human family"—Ed.], one *ecclesia universalis* ["universal church"—Ed.], with one law and one government. The main conflict of the Middle Ages was not between universalism and the desire of separation of individual groups, but between two forms of universalism, *Sacerdotium* and *Imperium*,[1] a struggle unknown in the Eastern Church and unknown in Islam, where universalism remained a reality much longer than in Western Christianity.

Although Islam was split up very soon into several kingdoms, often warring among themselves, the division of Islam was, like that of Christianity in the later Middle Ages, based upon dynasties and the personalities and actions of successful rulers, and sometimes upon geographic and ethnographic factors, never upon a feeling of nationalism. Down to the end of the nineteenth century, religion, with its unifying regulation of thought, social life, and attitudes, entirely dominated the private and public life of all Islamic countries. The universities of Islam kept their medieval character until late in the nineteenth century, and the unity of literature and education in all Islamic countries provided a strong bond for the educated classes. A Mohammedan in the nineteenth century, if asked about himself and his loyalties, would have answered that he was a Mohammedan and that his loyalty was due to Islam and to his prince, who was a Mohammedan prince. A Christian, in the Europe of the later Middle Ages, would have given a similar answer. This fact explains why, in the later Middle Ages, Western Christendom and Islam, facing each other as irreducible

---

[1] "The priesthood" or "the priestly function" and "secular political power," that is, church and state. —Ed.

enemies with similar missionary claims as universal religions, met as equals. They had then not only the fundamental attitudes of life in common, but also, among their educated classes, science and philosophy, chivalry and poetry. Only with the breakdown of medieval Christendom, from the early modern period down to most recent times, have the nations of Christendom and the lands of Islam ceased to meet as equals. Islam conserved the medieval form of life; Western Christendom threw it off, partly in the days of the Renaissance, and completely in the eighteenth century.

The position in the Eastern Church was different. There the *Sacerdotium* remained subordinated to the *Imperium.* State and Church formed a single unit like body and soul; the Church, although universal in its idea, was not universal in its organization. As an organization it was coextensive with the State, and sometimes it even remained and fulfilled certain functions as a separate organization, which are generally assumed by the state, when, in the vicissitudes of history, the state had ceased to exist. Lacking a universal organization, the Eastern Church could adapt itself much more easily to the existing ethnographic and historical divisions. Its role in the history of nationalism was fundamentally different from that of the Western Church. The universal claim of the Roman Empire survived and continued infinitely stronger in the West, with Pope and Emperor alike, than with the legitimate heir of the Roman Empire, the Byzantine monarch and his Patriarch of Constantinople. The Church in the West set itself above national distinctions, and the formation of nations, from the thirteenth to the sixteenth century, accordingly proceeded amid a struggle against the Church. In the East the national groupings and the national organization of the Church proceeded generally in harmony with one another. For this very reason there came no schism. In place of the rigid monarchic unity of the Western Church there was established a conception of synthetic unity, the consciousness of unity in multiformity, a vital sense of cohesion, coupled with the existence of an autonomous church in each state.

Closer even than in the Catholic Eastern Church was the connection between Church and ethnographic and historic divisions in the heretic churches of the East. In the Middle Ages the historical consciousness of Egyptians, Syrians, or Mesopotamians expressed itself, if at all, in theological formulas and disputations; but how little real strength this kind of national consciousness had, how far it was from any modern national integration, is shown by the fact that all these churches have dwindled away and are reduced today to a few thousand adherents. Some of them (for instance, the Maronite Church)[2] helped to preserve the ethnographic differentiation of their followers, supported in that by the geographic features of their country, high mountains and secluded valleys, and the difficulties of communication. All these churches are in the twentieth century undergoing deep changes as the result of the penetration of modern nationalism. The Eastern churches kept their medieval form, as Islam did, down to the threshold of the present time. Like Islam, they have been separated from the Western Church since early modern times by a deep gulf. West-

---

[2] The Maronite Church was founded in Syria *ca.* 400 A.D. Always defenders of the "Chalcedonian doctrine" in the various schisms and disputes within the Orthodox Church, the Maronites have managed to maintain their independence and today number more than one million, about half of whom live in Lebanon.—Ed.

ern Crusaders ravaged Constantinople and its churches in 1204 with far greater savagery and far greater contempt for its sanctuaries than the Turks ever did.

In Western Europe the universal claim of the Pope and the Empire of Charlemagne succeeded in forming out of the chaos produced by the Germanic tribes, a new civilization, "Europe" or "Occidental Christendom." It was built on the foundation of the later Roman universalism, it was a *renovatio* or *restitutio* ["renewal" or "restitution"—Ed.]. It dominated Western Europe for many centuries, until new forces, themselves a renaissance, prepared the ground for the later rise of nationalism. State and Church, Empire and Christianity were indissolubly linked. There was an all-dominating recognition of the necessity of a universal Empire, and this Empire was by necessity Christian and Roman at the same time. In no walk of life was there any separation of the secular and temporal from the eternal, which at the same time was the ecclesiastical. Man and his life on earth had their definite station in the cosmos of time and space, between Creation and Resurrection, between Heaven and Hell. The whole earthly life was overspanned by another, the eternal life, for which the years here on earth were only a preparation. Man's daily life, and the rise and fall of empires, were seen *sub specie aeternitatis* ["under the aspect of eternity"—Ed.].

An order thus firmly anchored in a supranatural unquestionable revelation not only gave a feeling of security and stability, unknown to the times following the Renaissance; it provided also for every problem of daily life, as well as for those of politics and philosophy, an unshakable frame of reference, common to every man and to every scholar. Civilization at that time was conventional. The accepted standards, methods, and usages were uniform, dominated by firm tradition, the foundation of which was entirely identical in all lands of Western Christendom. The whole cultural life was in the hands of the clergy, who formed not a separate caste but a body fundamentally different from the laity. They alone were entitled to administer or to withhold the holy sacraments which guaranteed the realization of the meaning of life and the salvation of man, living then in perpetual fear of damnation and Hell. The clergy had therefore the power of eternal life or eternal death.

These clerics formed one uniform and closely knit body all over Western Christendom. Latin, the language of its liturgy (the Bible was then used only in its Latin translation, the Vulgate), became the language of diplomacy, of officialdom, of literature, and of instruction. In character and privileges the clergy were entirely separated from the laity, but they renewed themselves constantly with new recruits from the ranks of the laity. The clergy offered to the gifted members of the lower classes the opportunity not only of access to scholarship and intellectual life, but also of rising above their station of life. The Church could have provided Western Christendom with a unique, highly organized and qualified leadership if the clergy had not been corrupted again and again by a greed for power, by worldliness and sensuality.

The official doctrine of the medieval Church was the doctrine of the renunciation of the world, of asceticism and of humility. This idea did not conflict with the establishment of the dominion of the Church over the world. If the world beyond was the chief goal of man, then the institution which in an authoritative manner disposed of the sacrament for salvation had to regulate life on earth in view of the future life. The Church imposed upon the unbroken instincts of primitive barbarians—their greed for earthly power and goods, their pride in fight and feud, their joy in strength and cunning—the stern demands of an ascetic humility and the higher notions of charity and self-discipline. But the lust of violence asserted itself against the spiritual yoke imposed upon it; chivalry and the Crusades offered the Church the possibility of restraining and of directing the love of violence and of slaughter.

Within the Church itself reform movements tried to revitalize the spirit of Christ according to his words (Matthew 10:7–10): "And as ye go, preach, saying, The kingdom of heaven is at hand. Heal the sick, cleanse the lepers, raise the dead, cast out devils: freely ye have received, freely give. Provide neither gold, nor silver, nor brass in your purses, nor scrip for your journey, neither two coats, neither shoes, nor yet staves, for the workman is worthy of his meat." These movements, centered in monasticism, originated in individual enthusiasm as a protest against the worldliness into which the Church had fallen. They themselves soon became lax, and sometimes ended in abuses worse than those they had combated. Then the figure of the monk became an object of popular derision and scorn. But new reform movements emerged again and again from the inspiration of the original message of self-surrender, of poverty, and of service. The great beginning made at Monte Cassino (529) was followed in the tenth century by the movement of Cluny, at the beginning of the twelfth century by St. Bernard's foundation at Clairvaux.

Finally, at the beginning of the thirteenth century, the point of the highest development of the Middle Ages, which necessarily enclosed the seeds of its dissolution and the first signs of the approach of a new age, the reform movement culminated in St. Francis, who invested poverty with a new dignity, and whose followers were absorbed in alleviating the misery of the poor in the Italian cities—the first Christian movement born in response to the new challenge thrown out by the rise of a new urban civilization with its wealth and its proletariat. From the ranks of the Franciscans (the Gray Friars) and of the Dominicans (the Black Friars) came the climax of medieval learning, a response to the challenge thrown out by the growth of science and philosophy transmitted by Arabs and Jews from the still undesiccated springs of Hellenism in the Near East. Albertus Magnus was born in Swabia, Thomas Aquinas near Naples, William Occam in Surrey;[3] all three studied and lived in Italy, in France, in Germany, representing the universalism of the Middle Ages in their descent and life as did their attempts to produce a synthesis of all knowledge, of the *sapientia Christiana* ["Christian wisdom"—Ed.], which was then one for the whole of Western Christendom.

Beneath this all-embracing and all-dominating universalism there throve an immensely rich and varied growth of local life, a bewildering and intricate juxtaposition, promiscuity, subordina-

---

[3] Albertus Magnus (1193–1280), a German Dominican, Doctor of the Church, Master of Theology at the University of Paris, and Professor of Theology at the University of Cologne; Thomas Aquinas (1225–1274), an Italian Dominican theologian, Doctor of the Church, Professor of Theology at the University of Paris, and author of the *Summa Theologica*, the greatest work of medieval scholasticism; William of Occam (*ca.* 1285–1347), an English Franciscan philosopher, theologian, and political writer. He taught for a time at Oxford but is best known for his exposition of nominalist philosophy and his polemical support of Louis of Bavaria.—Ed.

tion, and preeminence of institutions, jurisdictions, corporations—all of them self-sufficient to a very high degree. Many of these associations were voluntary, governed by customs and contract. The consequence was the division of the population into many classes, castes, and orders, with very little contact among them. No direct link brought government and people together; many intermediary institutions and organs provided a permanent check upon any central power and precluded the development of modern sovereignty. The universalism from above, the system of local and occupational autonomy from below, made nationalism impossible. Its growth could begin only when the universalism of the Middle Ages was definitely broken up and when the rising power of the kings forced the multifarious and intertangling loyalties to accept the supreme loyalty to the sovereign state and, with it, a new, though this time parochial, uniformity. . . .

Any feeling of national particularism in the later Middle Ages expressed itself as part of the universalism of the Empire. A separate national consciousness, a *Nationalbewusstsein* ["national consciousness"—Ed.] different from the universal *Reichsidee* ["concept of empire"—Ed.], was never imagined. Walther von der Vogelweide spoke of *daz roemische riche* and *diu tiusche zunge* ["the Roman empire", and "the German language"—Ed.] without making any definite difference or seeing any conflict between them. "As yet no German spirit existed, but only a Roman spirit which was gradually civilizing the Germanic. It was not common German tradition which bound the Northerners together, but Roman form and culture. The German races had nothing in common but

their blood, and the call of the blood was rarely vocal. Just now and then, . . . in solemn moments of enthusiasm, . . . they felt . . . that they—Saxons, Franks, Suabians and Bavarians—were one. But they did not even then feel 'German.' At most they felt that they stood together as heirs of the Empire of the Caesars, they prided themselves on being descendants of the Trojans, or styled themselves 'Roman' citizens. The word 'German' is reserved for our use today." Most characteristic was the charter of the Teutonic Order,[4] which by its conquests spread German dominion and colonization far to the east and northeast. "For this end has God uplifted our Empire above the kingdoms of the earth, and extended the limits of our power beyond the various zones, that our care may be to glorify His name and diligently to spread His faith among the people, for He has chosen the Roman Empire for the preaching of His gospel: Let us therefore bend our mind to the conquest, no less than to the conversion, of the heathen peoples. . . ."

The word *deutsch* was first employed in the eighth and ninth centuries to designate the German language. Only in the eleventh century did it begin to designate the people speaking the language, and their land. Its use did not imply the existence of a political national consciousness. The first flickering of a German consciousness in the masses, the German peasant revolt, was quickly and definitely crushed by the princes and nobles. The national consciousness which the German humanists developed from literary sources did not influence deeply the aristocracy and did

---

[4] One of the three great military-monastic orders founded during the Crusades, the Teutonic Order devoted its efforts primarily to expanding German power into Prussia and Poland.—Ed.

not reach the people. Though a consciousness of being different in language and appearance from other groups existed, the Germans continued until the seventeenth century, politically and culturally, to think exclusively within the frame of the universal Empire.

With the decline of the power of the Pope, German political ideas became detached from their connection with the locality of Rome, and centered territorially upon Germany. Louis of Bavaria[5] declared in 1338 that the election by the electors alone was sufficient to confer imperial dignity. Charles IV,[6] the grandson of Henry VII[7] and a monarch of wise and realistic statesmanship, abandoned the exuberant dreams of his grandfather, and devoted his energies to his own territory, the Bohemian kingdom, which he made the most progressive part of Central Europe by introducing the new learning from Italy and France.

The imperial idea detached itself in the fourteenth century from its "transcendent" centers, Rome and Jerusalem. The crusaders to the Holy Land faded out. The imperial idea was now closely connected with some definite territory: with Germany for the Germans, with France for the Frenchmen, with Italy and with contemporary Rome for the Italians. Spain was still absorbed in the task of the *reconquista,* and England, isolated by the sea, developed an early consciousness of territorial unity. For both of them only the sixteenth century ushered in their imperial era, which was no longer static, but dynamic — not turned to the past, but to the future and the unknown. But in the winds that blew over the immense ocean, enticing and seducing to strange and unheard-of lands, there was, for the English as well as for the Spaniards, a strong scent of the new Jerusalem and of eternal Rome. Without this scent the imperial venture would have seemed meaningless to the peoples of Western Christendom even long after the end of the Middle Ages.

In Eastern Christendom the position of the Byzantine Empire was rendered increasingly precarious by the successful progress of Islam, the great imperial heir of the ancient Hellenistic East. When Islam conquered Constantinople, in 1453, a new imperial claim was put forward by the princes of Moscow, who were united with the imperial house by ties of religion and of marriage. Moscow was now proclaimed the third Rome; its princes assumed the imperial two-headed eagle and the title Caesar. As the German barbarians were lured to Rome by its promises of higher civilization, of greater riches, of a kinder and more bountiful nature, so the barbarians of the cold Sarmatian plains were attracted by the similar promises of Constantinople. As the Empire of Charlemagne's successors strove for the possession of Rome, the great *Urbs,* so the Slavonic successors of the emperors longed for new Rome, the great *Polis* of Czarigrad, the traditional residence of the emperors. It remained the center of attraction and struggle on an imperial scale long after Rome had sunk politically to purely local significance. On the other hand, Rome remained the living center of the spiritual Empire of the Pope, giving up none of its universal claims, while Constantinople, like Jerusalem, became spiritually no more than a memory and a hope.

---

[5] Holy Roman Emperor, 1314–1347. Most of Louis' reign was spent in a dispute with the papacy over his claim to the throne. See note 3 above — Ed.

[6] Holy Roman Emperor, 1347–1378. — Ed.

[7] Holy Roman Emperor, 1308–1313. — Ed.

The distinguished Dutch cultural historian JOHAN
HUIZINGA (1872–1945) disputes Kohn's point that
nationalism did not exist in the Middle Ages. Indeed
Huizinga asserts that modern nationalism differs from
the medieval variety only in that the former is "more
clearly delineated." In his opinion the foundations of
nationalism were laid as early as 1100, and by the end
of the Middle Ages the sentiment associated with it had
gained considerable ground in all areas of European
society.*

Johan Huizinga

Nationalism in the Middle Ages

The opinion is widespread among historians and political scientists that both patriotism and national consciousness, not to mention present-day nationalism, are cultural phenomena of a recent date. The chief basis for the opinion is the fact that the words and the formulated concepts are themselves quite recent. The word "patriotism" first cropped up in the eighteenth century, and "nationalism" only in the nineteenth. In French *nationalisme* is to be found once in 1812; the oldest example of "nationalism" in English dates from 1836, and then, remarkably, with a theological significance, namely for the doctrine that certain nations have been chosen by God. Considering that "nationalism" later came to fill a larger sphere of significance in English than in Dutch (and than in French or German), the English word has carved a place for itself in the world in a single century.

The conclusion that the phenomena of patriotism and nationalism are recent because the words and concepts are recent is easily drawn, but misleading. It stems from the age-old human habit of attributing existence to things only once they have a name. On the same basis one might conclude that there were no cosmic rays in the Middle Ages. Or, to mention a more closely related parallel, on a similar basis—the lack of a name or a concept for

* Reprinted from Johan Huizinga, *Men and Ideas: History, the Middle Ages, the Renaissance,* translated by James S. Holmes and Hans van Marle, pp. 99, 102–109, 110–117. Copyright © 1959 by the Free Press, A Corporation. Translation Copyright © 1950 by Meridian Books. Reprinted by permission of Harper & Row, Publishers Inc. Footnotes omitted.

the matter at hand—the existence of the state in medieval times has been denied. It is true that the word and the concept "state" were only brought to the fore by the Renaissance, but even though the phenomenon "state" was largely hidden behind that of the Church in the Middle Ages, medieval society made good use of the concepts *regnum* and *civitas* ["kingdom" and "union of citizens," that is, commonwealth—Ed.] to express things political.

On close observation the equivalents of patriotism and nationalism prove to have been present in earlier periods, and more significantly, the only change in the two emotions in the course of time has actually been that they have become somewhat more clearly delineated. For the rest, they have remained what they always were: primitive instincts in human society. . . .

The Christian faith was raised above the confused contrasts of nations and kingdoms as early as the time of Saint Paul. It had no contact with questions of political allegiance or national entity, and left the state for what it was, rendering unto Caesar the things that were Caesar's. Nonetheless, the organization of the faith, the Church, required a political organization as a basis for its earthly task, and for its defenders "render unto Caesar" and "there is no power but of God" were not enough. A Christian theory of the state was indispensable. Hence Augustine constructed the tremendous edifice of his *De civitate Dei* [*The City of God*—Ed.], in which he was forced to assign to the secular state—in itself reprehensible—a dual function: that of being an emergency institution without which no human society, and no peace, was possible, and that of serving and protecting the Church for as long as this world shall last. The Roman Empire,

the last of the four world-empires of Daniel's vision, would continue for a while, purified and sanctified, in the *imperator christianus* ["Christian emperor"—Ed.]. As Augustine wrote his *De civitate* the authority of that emperor was collapsing, at least in the West, where the saint lived. It is no wonder, then, that in principle he preferred an international order in which "the kingdoms of the earth would have continued little in quantity, and peaceful in neighbourly concord. And then many kingdoms would have been in the world, as many families are now in a city." Here, for the first time, the principle of independent states living together in concord is clearly formulated. Before Augustine's century had reached its end, the West would indeed number many states that sooner or later were to become Christian, although not in quite the concord that Augustine had wished for. All of them held fast, as much as possible, to the tradition of Roman imperial authority, whether they were the Ostrogoths in Italy, the Visigoths on either side of the Pyrenees, the Vandals in Africa, or the Franks in Gaul. Then from the kingdom of the Franks there suddenly sounded the clarion call of a new national awareness in which, however contradictory it may seem, the glory of Christian salvation was intermingled with the primitive pride of a barbaric tribal allegiance. I am referring to the well-known prologue to the Salic law,[1] which, even though it may be slightly more recent than the law itself, nonetheless reflects the Merovingian situation. It speaks of "the glorious nation of the Franks" which traced its origins to God, "brave in arms, faithful in peace, wise in council," and ends with a triumphant cry:

---

[1] A fifth-century compilation of the laws of the Frankish tribes.—Ed.

Hail Christ, who loves the Franks. May He protect their kingdom, may He fill their leaders with the light of His grace, may He watch over their army, may He strengthen their faith, may He grant them joy and happiness! For this is the nation that with strength and bravery has shaken off the hard yoke of the Romans, and after its acceptance of Christianity has enshrined in buildings decked with gold and precious stones the bodies of the holy martyrs burnt, beheaded, and thrown to the wild beasts by the Romans.

European nationalism had started out on its path through history. The Christian West began its political evolution on a dual foundation: an ideal of a universal Christian world dominion, and a reality of as yet unsteady complexes of power, barbaric in nature and Roman in tradition. Gradually, over a period of a good six centuries, Latin Christendom arranged itself in a number of kingdoms corresponding, though still very roughly, to national lines. The neighborly concord that Augustine had set as a condition was absent, but the times were not yet ripe for major national wars. Except for occasional expeditions of conquest quite rapidly completed, violence was constant and intense, but on a small scale. Now what, in these earlier Middle Ages, was the result of the ideal of universal power above and beyond the multiplicity of separate states? It called into being both the restored imperium of Charlemagne and the supreme secular authority of the pope.

Customarily the medieval opposition of pope and emperor is viewed from the very outset in the light of the theory of the two powers as the two celestial bodies God had placed over the earth at the time of creation. This symbolism, however, was not applied to the imperium before the days of Frederick Barbarossa.[2] The emperors from Charlemagne onward had pretended to continue the Roman Empire, but not to wield universal dominion. That ideal was first to be heard when the Hohenstaufen ruler wrote to a bishop: "One God, one pope, one emperor, are enough for the world." The real power of the emperors never depended on that claim, nor on the title.

The claim of the pope to universal authority was much more one of principle than was that of the emperor, and in a certain sense it was also more effective. At first glance it seems pure hierarchical pride when Peter's successor demands the supreme right of authority over all nations and above all kings of the earth — besides the ultimate word in matters of dogma and of Church administration. Yet that demand stemmed directly from the heart of the Church's doctrine. The Holy See did not at all deny kings and princes their authority. It did, however, claim the right to judge each juridical and administrative act of the rulers in exercising that authority. The deeds of the kings continued to be subject to the power of the keys, according to the criterion of good and evil, *ratione peccati* ["for the reason of sin"]. But such a judgment of royal deeds by the criterion of religion unavoidably brought with it the criterion of justice. And hence from the time of Nicholas I[3] in the ninth century, one finds the doctrine of papal dominion over the world formulated ever more positively, and repeatedly put into practice in deposing kings, granting lands, and bypassing existing laws.

In this great conflict between the concepts of papal and imperial dominion there was no soil for a further development of national consciousness and the sense of a fatherland. On the other hand,

[2] Holy Roman Emperor, 1152–1190. — Ed.

[3] Pope Nicholas I, "the great," 858–867. — Ed.

the concepts did not serve to impede the evolution of the national configuration of Europe. The consolidation of the states and nations of the West had gradually continued after the collapse of Carolingian power. France, England, and Scotland, the three Scandinavian kingdoms, Aragon, Castile, and Portugal, Sicily, Hungary, and Poland had all of them taken their places as units of Latin Christianity by around 1150. The claims of the imperium, which was named after Rome and was in the hands of the Germans, were, in spite of the imperial authority, not able to prevent all those kings from demanding complete sovereignty—or in medieval terms, imperial dignity—for themselves. In exactly the same period when the struggle between the pope and the emperor for universal authority reached its height, shortly before 1200, the national organization of Europe had little by little become a fact. Saint Hildegard of Bingen[4] betrays a remarkable insight into this fact in her visions. While the two greatest universalists of the Middle Ages, Emperor Henry VI and Pope Innocent III, were still to come, she saw the imperial aspirations to world power retreating before the national principle:

In those days the rulers of the Roman Empire shall lose the strength with which they had earlier held that empire, grown powerless in their glory. The kings and princes of the many nations that hitherto were obedient to the Roman Empire shall detach themselves from it and no longer be subject thereto. And thus shall the Roman Empire be dispersed by default. For every region and every nation shall place itself under a king, whom it shall obey.

The framework within which national consciousness and a sense of fatherland were to evolve in Europe, then, was established by around 1100. How had the usage and significance of the words *patria* and *natio* ["fatherland" and "tribe," "race," or "people"—Ed.] developed meanwhile? The Latin terms must be taken as the points of departure, for it was in writings in Latin that the two concepts were formed. The word *patria* had not been lost with the end of the ancient period. The expression *caelestis patria*, the celestial fatherland, was of itself enough to keep the concept alive, and the word was to be found in the earthly sense in several places in the Old Testament. In that earthly sense, however, *patria* no longer had the full resonance of the ancient Roman word. It had become an administrative term without a great deal of emotional value. Such emotions did exist, as the *douce France* ["sweet France" —Ed.] of the *Chanson de Roland*[5] evinces, but they were not associated with the word *patria*. *Patria* was used to indicate a specific jurisdiction, a county or a group of several counties. It was the exact equivalent of *terra*, or in French *pays*, the word for the many regions that gave to pre-Revolutionary France so much more charming a pattern than the present-day checkerboard of departments. Hence in the twelfth and thirteenth centuries one repeatedly encounters phrases such as *tota patria congregatur*—the whole region, the entire land, is called together. A person is exiled from his *patria*. Naturally there was, as a rule, a correspondence between the limits of the jurisdiction and those of the native land that one was

---

[4] The mystic German Benedictine abbess of Rupertsberg (1098–1179), who wrote on the lives of saints, medicine, and natural history, and corresponded with the important political figures of her time.—Ed.

[5] "Song of Roland," a lyric poem, probably written in the late eleventh century, which commemorates the achievements of the "knights" of the time of Charlemagne.—Ed.

attached to with all the fondness the *Heimat* ["homeland"—Ed.] can inspire. Here, then, is the older, more restricted sense of a fatherland, or if one prefers, a feeling for one's native soil. Only in a few cases in these centuries can the word *patria* be found used in a different way, and then probably under the influence of classical reading. Gerbert, the renowned scholar of the late tenth century who was to become Pope Sylvester II, sometimes used *patria* in a more limited sense and sometimes in a broader one, but, remarkably, neither for Aquitaine, his native land, nor for Auvergne, his *pays* in the restricted sense, and certainly not for the kingdom of France as a whole. Gerbert lent a great deal of support to transferring the French crown from the Carolingian dynasty to the house of Hugh Capet.[6] Hence it is all the more surprising that his *patria* concept applied to the German emperors Otto II and Otto III,[7] whom he had faithfully served. And with him that *patria* has an almost classical or modern sound. He impresses upon Otto III that he should seek his renown in "braving the greatest dangers for the fatherland, for the faith, for the welfare of his people, and for the commonweal [*rei publicae salute*]". So little, one must conclude, were the French and the Germans aware of their factual political separation around the year 1000.

The word *natio* had always remained much more current than *patria*. Actually it had changed very little in connotation since classical Latin. Closely linked with *natus* and *natura* ["by birth" and "nature," that is, natural disposition—Ed.], it vaguely indicated a larger context than

gens or *populus* ["tribe" or "people" —Ed.], but without there being any fixed distinction between the three terms. The Vulgate used *gentes, populos,* and *nationes* interchangeably for the nations of the Old Testament, and that biblical usage determined the significance of *natio* for the time being. It indicated a fairly indefinite interrelationship of tribe, tongue, and region, sometimes in a restricted sense, sometimes in a broader one. The Burgundians, the Bretons, the Bavarians, and the Swabians were called nations, but so were the French, the English, and the Germans. Unlike *patria, natio* did not have an administrative significance, and initially not a political one either. But little by little the various relationships of dependence and community obtaining exerted an influence on the restriction and delimitation of the concept *natio*. The glory of the kingship, the fealty to the liege lord, the protection of the bishop, the mildness of the master, created a great number of relationships of close community. Only the larger relationships of this sort could be expressed by the term *natio*. But whether the relationship was large or small the basis for the emotion embodied in *natio* was the same everywhere: the primitive in-group that felt passionately united as soon as the others, outsiders in whatever way, seemed to threaten them or to rival them. This feeling usually manifested itself as hostility and rarely as concord. The closer the contacts the fiercer the hate. It is for this reason that there were no more violent enmities than those between neighboring towns, for instance the rivalry between Genoa and Pisa, which Salimbene[8] says in his chronicle were divided by a natural aversion such as that between

---

[6] King of France, 987–996, and founder of the Capetian dynasty, which ruled France 987–1328. —Ed.

[7] Otto II, Holy Roman Emperor, 973–983; Otto III, Holy Roman Emperor, 983–1002.—Ed.

[8] A thirteenth-century Italian Franciscan chronicler.—Ed.

men and snakes or wolves and dogs. The two noble cities, he states in his account of the naval battle of Meloria in 1284, destroyed each other out of sheer ambition, pride, and vanity "as if there were not sea enough to sail." The English hated the Scots, and the Danes the Swedes, in the same way, though perhaps less violently, as did also the French of the *langue di'oïl*[9] the Aquitanians. The form in which these emotions were expressed demonstrates their instinctive character. The eleventh-century French chronicler Radulf Gaber reproached King Robert I's[10] queen for opening France and Burgundy to the Aquitanians, vain and frivolous folk who were as affected in their ways as in their dress: they wore their hair cropped half long and shaved their beards like buffoons, wore improper stockings and shoes, and worst of all, they could not keep faith. Clearly their clothing was at least as irritating as their morals. This sort of thing can hardly be called political sentiment. Nor can the old, deep-seated antagonism between Romance and Germanic peoples which vaulted above all those local, regional, and national antagonisms actually be given such a label, for that antipathy was to be found even before the political division between the Romance and Germanic parts of the Carolingian empire had come about. The life of Saint Goar, written around 840 by the monk Wandalbert in the monastery of Prüm, in the Eifel, tells of a German living along the Rhine who

with a certain national hatred [*quodam gentilicio odio*] abhorred all persons of Romance nation and language [*Romanae nationis ac linguae*] so much that he was not even willing to view the face of one of them with equanimity. Such an obtuseness born of barbaric ferocity had seized his mind that he could not look upon people of Romance language or nation passing by—even upright, noble men—without aversion.

The lasting political foundation for this great ethnic antithesis was actually only laid in the year 887. The Verdun treaty of partition in 843 had been merely a solemn repetition of the partitions that were long since traditional in the Frankish empire, perpetuating the unity of the empire in name. Only after Charles the Fat[11] had failed in an attempt to restore that unity in actuality did the definitive partition between an East Frankish and a West Frankish realm become a fact. *Hic divisio facta est inter Teutonicos et Latinos Francos*, says the official chronicle regarding the treaty of 887: "Here was the division made between the Germanic and the Romance Franks." From that time on there was a Germany and a France. When early in the tenth century Charles the Simple[12] met Henry,[13] soon afterward to become king of the Germans, at Worms, the young noblemen of both retinues, *linguarum idiomate offensi* ["offended by the idiom of each others' languages"] occupied themselves, as was their custom (says the Richer chronicle), with heaping violent contumely upon each other, then drawing their swords and fighting one another to the death— a peacemaker was one of the victims.

The Crusades, far from uniting in the faith what was divided by language, descent, and allegiance, reinforced the na-

---

[9] The *langue d'oïl* was the Romance dialect of northern France. The reference here is to the hostility between the northern French *(langue d'oïl)* and those who lived in the southern provinces *(langue d'oc)*. —Ed.

[10] King of France, 922–923. —Ed.

---

[11] King of the Franks and Emperor, 884–887. —Ed.

[12] King of the West Franks, 893–923. —Ed.

[13] The later Henry I, "the Fowler," king of Germany, 919–936. —Ed.

tional enmities of the peoples of Latin Christendom by bringing those peoples together again and again in martial equipment, battle array, and a more or less sanctified rivalry. Eckhart of Aura[14] speaks of the hostility between the German and French knights in the First Crusade as an *invidia quae inter utrosque naturaliter quodammodo versatur* ["invidiousness that comes about between the two somewhat naturally"]. On the same occasion Guibert de Nogent[15] displays Germans, Lombards, and Sicilians joined together against the French, whose pride they could not abide. Himself a Frenchman, he adds, remarkably, that the French tend to behave themselves intractably among foreigners if they are not kept well in hand. . . .

It does not seem exaggerated to say that in the medieval West conscious political nationalism first appeared as a reaction to the German imperial policy of the Hohenstaufens.[16] A century later, the final result of the emperors' long and bitter struggle against the power of the pope, the towns and princes of Germany and Italy, and the increasing authority of the French king was that, together with the proud house of Hohenstaufen, that imperial policy had succumbed. In the continuing process of organizing Europe along national lines, it was henceforth for many centuries France and England, and later also Spain, that took the lead. The national antithesis between the Romance and the Germanic nations re-

mained what it had always been: a contrast in culture founded on the primitive basis of linguistic and ethnic differences. The contrast led to political hostility only in cases where neighbors on the two sides came into conflict with each other, such as that of the Flemish and the French, when the Leliaerts had to pronounce the difficult Dutch words *schild en vriend* ["shield and friend"] in Bruges in 1302, and when the Dutch poet Jacob van Maerlant[17] wrote his *wat wals is, vals is* ["everything Romance is false"]. The derivatives of the Old Teutonic word *walh* (Walloon, Valaisian, Welsh, Vlach) of course had several different meanings, depending on whether they were applied to French, Italians, or what not, just as did the derivatives of *diota* (Dutch, *diets, deutsch,* Teutonic), which could cover the whole range of Low and High German lands. The suggestive power of that antithesis *diota* and *walh* was so strong that Jan van Boendale[18] could simply ignore all the other nations of Europe when he wrote:

> Kerstenheit es gedeelt in tween:
> die Walsche tonge die es een,
> d'andre die Dietsche al geheel.[19]

There was only one place from which the national structure of Europe that had gradually developed was clearly seen: from the *curia* of the Holy See. Rome was in constant touch with all those lands and peoples, yet was above and beyond their multiplicity. Only in Rome could there actually be a question of international politics in practice, and as a result of the papacy's knowledge of affairs and wide-

---

[14] A contemporary German chronicler of the First Crusade. — Ed.

[15] French ecclesiastic and historian of the First Crusade who wrote the *Gesta Dei per Francos.* Guibert lived *ca.* 1064–*ca.* 1125. — Ed.

[16] This family furnished most of the emperors of the Holy Roman Empire from 1137 until 1254. Often in conflict with the papacy, the Hohenstaufens were viewed as a "viper breed" by most popes of the period. — Ed.

[17] (*ca.* 1235–*ca.* 1291). Jacob is often referred to as "the father of Dutch poetry." — Ed.

[18] Dutch poet and moralist (1285–1365). — Ed.

[19] "Christendom is divided in twain: / The Romance tongue it is one, / The other all the Germanic tongues." — Ed.

spread sources of constant information, its diplomacy was far in advance of that of the secular states. Meanwhile, the organization of administrative systems in the other countries had become more efficient by around 1300. Unity of the state had become a conscious requirement, and in France and England the administrative, judicial, and financial systems had gained enough hold to provide the basis for a vigorous national policy. And there resounded a nationalism which in its ardor and energy concedes little to modern forms, one which was at the same time based on quite real political situations and aspirations, admixed with or disguised by Christian political ideals of a general kind. The crusades were over, that is to say, the power of the Latins in the Holy Land had been broken, but reconquest—thus the Crusade as a political concept—remained the recognized, prescribed objective of every Christian prince. Soon after 1300 Pierre Dubois, a lawyer from Normandy, wrote two political tracts, the first under the title "On the Curtailment of the Wars and Controversies of France," in which he advocated a general system of peace, with sanctions, boycotts, the intervention of neutrals, and so forth; and later one entitled "On the Reconquest of the Holy Land," in which he anticipated a hegemony of France for the benefit of Christendom. He was a zealous Frenchman. The Italian, in particular, was an object of his hatred. The French, he believed, had never received their just due: France was the logical leader for the Crusade, the pope should relinquish his secular power to the French king, and it would be to the advantage of the whole world to be subject to France because the French nation used more common sense than any other.

This, then, is political nationalism in full flower. A similarly proud and drastic nationalism on the part of England inspired the first prolonged conflict between two of the great national states of Europe, the Hundred Years' War between England and France.

In both countries the national consciousness was consolidated along with the growth of the state itself, and became a clear-cut factor in political life. This was not possible in the countries where a central power and a unified state did not develop: in Germany and Italy. In Germany neither the monarchy nor the imperium was capable of functioning as an active agent toward a politically potent awareness of a general Germanic nation and state. The last great Hohenstaufen, Frederick II, had already allowed suzerainty over the German princes, lords, and towns to pass out of his hands. A live general sense of Germanness definitely continued to exist, but it broke down, either as a loyalty to a clan, a region, or a town, or as a purely dynastic feeling through the countless units into which the Holy Roman Empire gradually threatened to dissolve. Thus it lost its political character, remaining on the intuitive level of sheer sentiment for the *Heimat*.

In Italy as well, every potential principle of national political unification had fallen short. Neither the old Lombard monarchy of the iron crown, the Sicilian kingdom of the Normans and the Hohenstaufens, nor the French adventure in power politics which carried the Anjous to Naples had been the starting point for a strong administration over all Italy and a corollary sense of national unity. Papal policy had deliberately blocked such a development rather than aiding it. Venice, Genoa, Florence, Milan, and all the other larger and smaller urban signories were most violently hostile and jealous toward one another. Nonetheless, amid all the factions a general Italian national consciousness continued to grow. The designations Rome and Italy never lost the resonance of a glorious past. The classical tradition was at all times stronger there than anywhere else, and that tradition implied unity. Simultaneous with the presumptuous French nationalism of Philip IV's[20] audacious policies, the note of an Italian patriotism and nationalism was sounded, never to fade again, for it was sounded in Dante's voice. It was in a minor key, for it lived in repression: *Ahi serva Italia, di dolore ostello* ["Thou inn of sorrow, ah, trampled Italy"]. . . . The idea of a liberated and reunited Italy became associated with the old dream of Roman universal dominion. An emperor of peace would bring to Italy the unity and tranquility that Dante cherished above all else. World dominion, *monarchia,* was the order God willed on earth. The people of Rome were destined to elect the emperor. And lo, Henry VII, the German emperor, came to fulfill his task of peace in Italy, and failed from the very outset. He died there in disillusionment, and lives forever in one of the highest spheres of Dante's *Paradiso.*

In quel gran seggio a che tu gli occhi tieni
   Perla corona che già v'è su posta
   Prima che tu a queste nozze ceni
Sedera l'alma che fia giù agosta
   Dell' alto Arrigi ch'a drizzare Italia
   Verrà in prima ch'ella sia disposta.[21]

Less than thirty years after Dante's death the fiery, poetic, mystical Italian patriotism and universalism that Dante had dreamed of in his *De monarchia* was made reality, as if in a wondrous, fantastic interlude in history, by the tribune of the people, Cola di Rienzi,[22] for half a year the liberator of Rome calling for the unity of Italy and the foundation of the universal empire, then for seven years an exile, a prisoner, and a political propagandist of a bad sort, finally to be exalted again in Rome, this time by papal policy, and to be killed in a street riot. The ideal of popular government, the classical freedom of the senate and the people, the glory of Rome, a pride in Italy, and a sacred aspiration for universal peace have never been so strangely combined as in that small, vain, faithless man Cola di Rienzi, whose only greatness was his dream.

There were two fields outside direct political and hierarchical relationships where the peoples of Europe constantly came into contact with one another in a manner forcing them to association and understanding on the basis of mutual trust. One was trade, the other was study —that is to say, the university. For the further development of the concept of nation both were fruitful, and particularly the latter. In the important commercial centers where merchants from everywhere assembled (Bruges is for the Dutchman the most familiar type), the foreign traders united into "nations." These "nations" undoubtedly served to strengthen the sense of national cohesion, but their field of activity was generally limited to the town harboring them.

The effect of the national principle was much more intensive and general in the universities that sprang up from the

---

[20] King of France, 1285–1314.—Ed.

[21] "On that great seat thine eyes are drawn unto/ By the crown hung already over it/Ere at this wedding-feast thyself art due,/The soul, on earth imperial, shall sit/Of the high Henry, coming to enforce/Right ways on Italy, though she is yet unfit."—Ed.

[22] (*ca.* 1313–1354). A Roman revolutionary of humble origin, Cola di Rienzi established a short-lived dictatorship in Rome in 1347–1348 and again in 1354.—Ed.

twelfth century onward in Italy, Spain, France, and England, and soon found in Paris their indisputable *primus inter pares* ["first among equals"—Ed.]. *Studium* ["application to learning," that is, the educational function—Ed.] was highly honored in the Middle Ages; sometimes it was posed as an equal member of a trinity along with *sacerdotium,* the office of the Church, and *imperium,* that of the state. Ecclesiastical authority reigned supreme in the university. Masters and scholars were clerics. The school as such was strictly international, and its instruction, in the liberal arts, theology, ecclesiastical and secular laws, and medicine, was not generally made subservient to any political or national interest. University life, however, led from the very outset to national grouping. The scholars, a turbulent mass of largely foreign, mostly poor, and always young persons, were an element of constant friction with the people among whom they were living. They often had to depend on each other for the safeguarding of their rights and their existence. What was more natural than that they should form groups according to their *natio,* either in the older, narrower sense of the region where they were born or in the broader sense of the state or realm to which they were bound by laws, language, and customs? The university became a starting point and a focal point for national organization. In Bologna, the university itself in a certain sense grew out of the combination of national student *corporationes,* each of which had before called itself *universitas.* As is known, up to that time the term *universitas* had meant nothing more than a community, a "corporation," of whatever sort. The scholars of Bologna were divided into two large groups, the Cismontanes, including the "nations" of the Lombards, Tuscans, and Romans, and the

Tramontanes or Ultramontanes, in the beginning consisting of no less than fourteen different "nations."

In Paris, also, an initial grouping in numerous "nations" soon gave way to four larger ones: the French, the Picards, the Norman, and the English. Three of these thus represented regions of northern France, while the fourth, the *natio Anglica* ["English nation"—Ed.], not only included everyone coming from the British Isles, whether he spoke English, Anglo-French, or one of the Celtic languages, but also had to accommodate Germans, Scandinavians, Poles, and what not. Here, then, there was an instability in the concept *natio* which was bound to lead to conflict in the course of time. Only in the middle of the fourteenth century was a *natio Alemanniae* ["German nation"—Ed.] split off from the *natio Angliae;* it was in turn quickly subdivided in a Low German and a High German nation.

At the English universities of Oxford and Cambridge the jealousy and the often bloody wrangling that was in many ways the distinctive element of the "nations" was, to say the least, no less evident than elsewhere. At Oxford the very statutes stipulated an official division into two "nations," strangely enough not on the basis of the differences between England, Wales, and Ireland (Scotland was not involved), but of that between northern and southern England. Wherever universities developed in the following period, for instance in the German lands, the system of "nations" was adopted. Under their procurators, chosen for a brief period from among the young masters of arts, the nations were the most unsettled part of the university. The system furthered the penetration of a national consciousness in very broad circles in every country and at the same time preserved the international character of the whole.

Ecclesiastical organization had long been on the way toward a certain process of nationalization. England, in particular, had achieved an important amount of autonomy in Church affairs as early as the thirteenth century. The popes themselves were the first to make use of the national principle, as a counterweight to the power of the college of cardinals, when the archbishops and bishops at the Council of Lyons in 1274 met by nations alongside of, and in opposition to, the cardinals. Final voting at the Council of Vienne in 1311–12 was held nation by nation. It seemed as if the Great Schism that began in 1378 would accelerate the disaggregation of the Church. Each land chose sides for the pope at Rome or the pope at Avignon. And when the Council of Pisa was finally convened in 1409 to restore the unity of the Church, the principle of the nations was indisputably master. The four nations of Italy, France, Germany, and England constituted the formal organization of the council. Dissolving without having reached a solution, the council met again five years later at Constance. There the principle of the nations gave rise to a serious controversy. The English and the Germans wanted to retain it; Cardinal d'Ailly[23] opposed it. England refused a fifth place, after Aragon as fourth, and had its way, because King Sigismund's[24] diplomacy led him to

England's side. Several points deserve particular attention in this connection. In the first place, that the *natiounes* at the council were considered to be representatives of the whole population of their country. Secondly, that the nations did not completely correspond to the existing states. Representatives from Savoy, Provence, and a large part of Lorraine voted with the French, though all those lands were still considered to be part of the Holy Roman Empire. What, then, characterized a nation as such? Language, dynastic bonds, ecclesiastical ties? The question was debated, without agreement being reached. There was, however, a dawning awareness that a difference existed between general nations and specific nations—which in turn produced new points of disagreement. Men such as Cardinal d'Ailly were fully aware how dangerous for the unity of the Church the recognition of the nations as the elements of Christendom could become.

The council convening in Basel in 1431 as the last of the series allowed the authority of the nation-principle in Church affairs to lapse in its futile discussions. But at the same time the reunified papacy was busy arriving at compromises with the larger countries which confirmed the already far advanced nationalization of the Church as a fact. Gallicanism and Anglicanism were just around the corner.

Toward the end of the Middle Ages, then, the forces of patriotism and nationalism were winning more and more ground in Church and state alike, and no less so in popular life and culture.

---

[23] Pierre d'Ailly (1350–1420), French scholastic theologian and cardinal who played an important role in the conciliar movement of the early fifteenth century.—Ed.

[24] Holy Roman Emperor, 1410–1437.—Ed.

To the French medievalist MARC BLOCH (1886–1944), history should be written as the story of "how and why people live and work together." He attempted in all of his writing to integrate political, economic, legal, and intellectual history into a narrative that would describe the total society of an age. It has been the conclusion of many historians that he was successful in this effort in *Feudal Society,* the source from which the present selection is taken. Note the wide range of time and area Bloch covers in developing his thesis.*

Marc Bloch

Medieval National Consciousness

As a reaction against romantic historiography, it has been the fashion among some recent historians to deny that the early centuries of the Middle Ages had any group consciousness at all, either national or racial. This is to forget that in the crude and naive form of antagonism to the stranger, the "outsider" *(horsin),* such sentiments did not require a very great refinement of mind. We know today that they manifested themselves in the period of the Germanic invasions with much more strength than Fustel de Coulanges,[1] for example, believed.

[1] A nineteenth-century French historian who stressed the strength and continuation of Roman ideas and institutions in the early Middle Ages. —Ed.

In the greatest example of conquest offered by the feudal era—that of Norman England—we see them clearly at work. When the youngest son of William, Henry I, had by a characteristic gesture, judged it a shrewd move to marry a princess of the ancient dynasty of Wessex— of the "direct" line of England, as it was called by a monk of Canterbury—the Norman knights took a derisive pleasure in loading the royal couple with Saxon nicknames. But singing the praises of this marriage, about half a century later, in the reign of the grandson of Henry and Edith, a hagiographer wrote: "Now England has a king of English race; it finds among the same race bishops, ab-

*From Marc Bloch, *Feudal Society,* translated by L. A. Manyon (2 vols.; University of Chicago Press, 1964), vol. 2, pp. 432–437. Reprinted by permission of the University of Chicago Press and Routledge & Kegan Paul Ltd. Translated from the French *La Société Féodale.* English translation © Routledge & Kegan Paul Ltd. 1961. Footnotes omitted.

bots, barons, brave knights, born of both seeds." The history of this assimilation, which is the history of English nationality, cannot be recounted here even in outline, owing to limitations of space. Leaving aside acts of conquest, it is within the boundaries of the former Frankish Empire, to the north of the Alps, that we must be content to examine the formation of national entities—the birth, so to speak, of France and Germany.

Here, of course, the tradition was unity —a relatively recent tradition, it is true, and to some extent an artificial one, as regards the Carolingian Empire as a whole; but within the narrower limits of the old *regnum Francorum* ["kingdom of the Franks"—Ed.], many centuries old and based on a real community of civilization. However palpable the differences of manners and language at the lower levels of the population, it was the same aristocracy and the same clergy which had helped the Carolingians to govern the vast state from the Elbe to the Atlantic Ocean. Moreover it was these great families, linked by ties of kinship, which after 888 had provided the kingdoms and principalities resulting from the dismemberment with their rulers, who were only superficially national. Franks disputed the crown of Italy; a Bavarian had assumed that of Burgundy; the successor to the West Frankish throne (Odo) was perhaps of Saxon origin. In the wanderings to which they were committed either by the policy of the kings (to whom they looked for rewards) or by their own ambitions, the magnates took with them a whole body of dependants; with the result that the vassal class itself shared this—so to speak—supra-provincial character. To contemporaries the laceration of the Empire in 840–843 naturally had the appearance of civil war.

Nevertheless, beneath this unity there survived the memory of older groups; and in a divided Europe it was these that first reasserted themselves, in mutual expressions of contempt or hatred. The Neustrians, exalted by their pride in coming from "the noblest region in the world," are quick to describe the Aquitanians as "perfidious" and the Burgundians as "poltroons"; the "perversity" of the "Franks" is denounced in its turn by the Aquitanians, and Swabian "deceit" by the people of the Meuse; a dark picture of Thuringian cowardice, Alemannian rapine, and Bavarian avarice is painted by the Saxons, all of course fine fellows who never run away. It would not be difficult to augment this anthology of abuse with examples drawn from writers ranging from the end of the ninth century to the beginning of the eleventh. . . . antagonisms of this type were particularly deep-rooted in Germany. Far from helping the monarchic states, they were a threat to their unity. The patriotism of the chronicler-monk Widukind, in the reign of Otto I, was certainly not wanting in fervour or intransigence; but it was a Saxon, not a German, patriotism. What effected the transition from this attitude to a consciousness of nationality adjusted to the new political framework?

It is not easy to form a clear picture of a fatherland without a name. Nothing is more instructive than the difficulty which men so long experienced in giving names to the two principal states carved out of the *regnum Francorum* by the partitions. Both were "Frances"; but the adjectives East and West by which they were long distinguished were not well fitted to evoke national consciousness. As for the labels Gaul and Germania, which a few writers at an early date sought to revive, they meant little except to the learned. Moreover, they did not correspond to the new frontiers. Recalling that Caesar had made the Rhine the frontier of Gaul, the German chroniclers frequently applied this name to their own provinces on the left bank. Sometimes, unconsciously emphasizing the original artificiality of the boundaries, men fastened on the memory of the first sovereign for whose benefit the kingdom had been carved out: to their neighbours in Lorraine and adjoining territories the Franks of the West remained the men of Charles the Bald *(Kerlinger, Carlenses)* just as the Lorrainers themselves were the men of the obscure Lothar II. German literature long remained faithful to this terminology, probably because it was reluctant to acknowledge the western people's monopoly of the name of Franks or French—the *Chanson de Roland* still employs the two terms indifferently—to which all the successsor states seemed to have a legal right.

As everyone knows, however, this restriction of meaning did take place; even at the time of the *Chanson de Roland* the Lorraine chronicler Sigebert of Gembloux regarded it as generally accepted. How did it come about? This great riddle of the French national name has not yet been adequately studied. The usage seems to have been implanted at the time when —in face of an East Frankish kingdom ruled by Saxons—the western kingdom returned to the authentic Frankish dynasty, the Carolingian line. It found support in the royal title itself. By contrast with his rivals who in their charters called themselves simply kings, Charles the Simple, after his conquest of Lorraine, had resumed the old title of *rex Francorum* ["king of the Franks"—Ed.] in order to proclaim his dignity as the heir of Charlemagne. His successors, although they now reigned only over France as we know it today, continued to parade the title more and more generally, even when

they had ceased to belong to the ancient line of kings. What is more, in Germany the name "Franks," as against other tribal groups, preserved almost of necessity a particularist character; it served in current usage to describe the people of the riparian dioceses and the valley of the Main—the region we call today Franconia—and a Saxon, for example, would scarcely have agreed to let himself be so described. On the other side of the frontier, however, there was nothing to prevent the term from being applied, if not to the entire population of the kingdom, at least to the inhabitants of the region between Loire and Meuse whose customs and institutions continued to be profoundly marked with the imprint of the Franks. Finally, the name was the more easily restricted to the France of the west, because the other France was by a natural process coming to be known by a very different name.

There was a striking contrast between "Charles's men" and the people of the eastern kingdom—a linguistic contrast, overriding the differences of dialect within each group—in that the language of the former was Romance and that of the latter *diutisc.* This adjective is the word from which the modern German *deutsch* is derived, but at that time in the Latin of the clergy, which abounded with classical memories, it was frequently rendered, in defiance of etymology, by "Teutonic." There is no doubt as to its origin. The *theotisca lingua* mentioned by the missionaries of the Carolingian age was none other, in the literal sense, than the speech of the people *(thiuda),* as opposed to the Latin of the Church; perhaps it was also the language of the pagans, the "Gentiles." Now since the term "German," a learned rather than a popular one, had never been deeply rooted in the general consciousness, the label thus devised to describe a mode of speech very soon rose to the dignity of an ethnic name—"the people speaking *diutisc*" is a phrase used already in the reign of Louis the Pious[2] in the prologue to one of the oldest poems written in that language. From this it was an easy step to its employment as the name of a political entity. Usage probably settled the matter long before writers ventured to give recognition to a development so little in accordance with traditional historiography. As early as 920, however, the Salzburg annals mention the kingdom of the Theotisci (or Teutons).

These facts will perhaps surprise those who are inclined to regard emphasis on language factors as a recent symptom of national consciousness. But the linguistic argument in the hands of politicians is not confined to the present day. In the tenth century a Lombard bishop, indignant at the claims—historically well founded—of the Byzantines to Apulia, wrote: "that this region belongs to the kingdom of Italy is proved by the speech of its inhabitants."

The use of the same language draws men closer together; it brings out the common factors in their mental traditions and creates new ones. But a difference of language makes an even greater impact on untutored minds; it produces a sense of separation which is a source of antagonism in itself. In the ninth century a Swabian monk noted that the "Latins" made fun of Germanic words, and it was from gibes about their respective languages that there arose, in 920, an affray between the escorts of Charles the Simple and Henry I so bloody that it put an end to the meeting of the two sovereigns. Moreover, within the West Frankish kingdom, the curious course of develop-

ment (not yet adequately explained) which had led to the formation within the Gallo-Romanic tongue of two distinct language groups meant that for long centuries the "Provençaux" or people of Languedoc, though without any sort of political unity, had a clear sense of belonging to a separate community. Similarly, at the time of the Second Crusade, the knights of Lorraine, who were subjects of the Empire, drew near to the French, whose language they understood and spoke. Nothing is more absurd than to confuse language with nationality; but it would be no less foolish to deny its role in the crystallization of national consciousness.

The texts make it plain that so far as France and Germany were concerned this consciousness was already highly developed about the year 1100. During the First Crusade Godfrey of Bouillon who, as a great Lotharingian noble, was fortunate enough to speak both languages, was hard put to it to control the hostility which, we are told, was already traditional between the French and German knights. The "sweet France" of the *Chanson de Roland* was present in all memories—a France whose frontiers were still a little uncertain, so that it was easily confused with the vast Empire of the Charlemagne of legend, but whose centre was unmistakably situated in the Capetian kingdom. Moreover, among men easily elated by conquests, national pride drew greater strength from being as it were gilded by the memory of the Carolingians; the use of the name "France" favoured the assimilation, and the legend in its turn helped to fix the name. (The Germans for their part took great pride in the fact that they were still the imperial people.) Loyalty to the crown helped to keep these sentiments alive: it is significant that they are almost completely absent from the

---

[2] Louis VII, king of France, 1137–1180.—Ed.

epic poems of purely baronial inspiration, like the cycle of Lorraine. We must not suppose, however, that the identification was complete. The monk Guibert de Nogent who, in the reign of Louis VI, wrote a history of the Crusade under the famous title of *Gesta Dei per Francos* ["The Deeds of God through the Franks"—Ed.] was an ardent patriot, but only a very lukewarm admirer of the Capetians. Nationality was nourished by more complex factors—community of language, of tradition, of historical memories more or less well understood; and the sense of a common destiny imposed by political boundaries each of which, though fixed largely by accident, corresponded as a whole to far-reaching and long-established affinities.

All this had not been created by patrio-tism; but in the course of the second feudal age, which was characterized both by men's need to group themselves in larger communities and by the clearer general consciousness of itself which society had acquired, patriotism became as it were the outward manifestation of these latent realities, and so in its turn the creator of new realities. Already, in a poem a little later than the *Chanson de Roland,* "no Frenchman is worth more than he" is the praise accorded to a knight particularly worthy of esteem. The age whose deeper history we are endeavouring to trace not only witnessed the formation of states; it also saw true fatherlands confirmed or established—though these were destined still to undergo many vicissitudes.

A specialist in feudal society and its institutions and author of numerous books and articles on feudalism, JOSEPH R. STRAYER (b. 1904), Dayton-Stockton Professor of History at Princeton University, here considers the gradual transformation of public attitudes in the late thirteenth century and relates this development to our larger issue of nationalism. In the process, he advances several interesting conclusions concerning when, why, and how it came into being.*

Joseph R. Strayer

Laicization and Nationalism in the Thirteenth Century

Students of mediaeval society have long been aware of a sharp change in attitudes and values which took place in the thirteenth century. During that period, while Europe remained sincerely and completely Catholic, the church lost much of its influence. Though it perfected its organization and carried on its religious activities with great energy, the standards which it had set for secular activities were increasingly disregarded. The forces released by the great revival of civilization in the twelfth century could no longer be controlled by the church. They broke out of the old channels and either found new courses for themselves or dissipated their energy in the swamps and backwaters of uncoordinated endeavor. This secularization of European society is apparent in every field of human activity, in art and literature as well as in politics and economics. But while the fact of secularization is undisputed, the reasons for this great change in European opinion and the way in which the change was brought about are not clear. It is a problem which is well worth studying, not only because it is the key to much of the later history of the middle ages, but also because it is an interesting example of the ways in which public opinion is changed.

This paper is an attempt to study one aspect of secularization, the laicization

* From Joseph R. Strayer, "The Laicization of French and English Society in the Thirteenth Century," *Speculum,* XV (1940), 76–86. Reprinted by permission of the Mediaeval Academy of America. Footnotes omitted.

of French and English society in the thirteenth century. Laicization may be defined as the development of a society in which primary allegiance is given to lay governments, in which final decisions regarding social objectives are made by lay governments, in which the church is merely a private society with no public powers or duties. When society has been laicized leadership has passed from the church to the state. In the modern period this assumption of leadership by the state is usually manifested in attempts to control social services, such as education, to regulate family relationships, and to confiscate all, or part of the church's property. These particular manifestations of the idea of laicization should not be confused with the idea itself. There was no demand for government regulation of marriage and divorce in the thirteenth century and very little protest against church control of education. There were efforts to limit the church's acquisition of new property, but only a few fanatics advocated confiscation of what the church already possessed. Yet during the thirteenth century leadership passed from the church to lay governments, and when the test came under Boniface VIII it was apparent that lay rulers, rather than the pope, could count on the primary allegiance of the people.

Laicization is the political aspect of secularization. As such, it cannot be wholly explained by purely economic factors. I am quite willing to accept the conventional view that the economic changes of the twelfth and thirteenth centuries made society more worldly, but worldliness is not the same thing as laicization. One is negative, the other positive. Worldliness made the leadership of the church less effective but it did not necessarily create a new leadership to supplant that of the church. Gothic art,

for example, did not express religious ideas as well in 1300 as it did in 1200, yet it was still an art dominated by the church. Society was more worldly everywhere in 1300 than in 1200, yet the church did not lose political power to the same extent everywhere. Germany was fully as worldly as England, yet England was far more independent of the papacy. It took strong lay governments to challenge the leadership of the church, and economic change by itself does not explain the development of such governments. For example, throughout Europe the new economic forces were concentrated in the towns, but outside of Italy the towns were not the dominant factor in creating the new leadership. In England and France the royal officials who were most active in pursuing the policy of laicization were not exclusively, or even primarily, bourgeois. In short, while economic changes created an atmosphere in which it was easier for lay governments to assume leadership, they did not ensure the creation of lay governments which could make the most of the opportunity.

A discussion of laicization really should be prefaced by a discussion of the way in which the church had obtained the leadership of society. For the church's leadership was not unquestioned in the earliest centuries of the middle ages. It may even be argued that the complete predominance of the church was attained only as a result of the great revival of civilization which began in the latter part of the eleventh century. Limitations of space forbid the discussion of this problem; at least we can assume that in the twelfth century the church's control of society reached its highest point. Disregarding the endless variations of a pattern which was everywhere fundamentally the same, we can say that political units of the twelfth century fell into three classes.

First, there were the local units, the feudal baronies and the towns. Then there were the intermediate units, the kingdoms, and the great feudal states which were practically independent. Finally there was the great unit of Christendom, headed nominally by the emperor and the pope, but which, as an effective political force, was almost wholly controlled by the pope. All men were subject to at least three governments, which represented these three types of political organization. No government had a monopoly of power, each had its own work to do and each was supposed to give the other governments a free hand to do their work. In practice there were endless quarrels, especially among the local and intermediate units, but for a long time these quarrels led to no decisive changes. This was a situation which, from a political point of view, was wholly favorable to the church. Loyalty to lay governments was divided between the local and intermediate units. In many cases the greater loyalty was to the small local unit, for it was the local unit which controlled economic and social status. Far more important than this divided allegiance to lay governments was the loyalty to the great undivided unit of Christendom. The scale of allegiance of most men would have gone something like this: I am first of all a Christian, second a Burgundian, and only third a Frenchman. The emphasis on Christianity as the most important bond between men meant that there was a real European patriotism, expressed in the armies of the Crusade. It means that there was such a thing as European citizenship or nationality, shown by the fact that a well-trained clerk or knight could find employment anywhere in Christendom, regardless of his origin. And the pope controlled the citizens of Europe and through this control he could exercise decisive influence on all aspects of European society.

From a political point of view this situation was satisfactory to the church. From the point of view of morality there was less reason for complacency. The division of responsibility between governments meant that none of them did their work very well. The quarrels between lay governments created a chronic state of warfare. This was intolerable to a church which had been preaching the ideals of peace and justice for centuries. The church was bound to support, or at least to look favorably on any reforms which would make lay governments more capable of enforcing peace and dispensing justice. Here the contrast between political and economic change is most apparent. From the very beginning the church was suspicious of the increase in business activities, and did nothing to aid it. On the other hand the church wanted more efficient lay governments, and was of great assistance in the development of such governments. Yet stronger lay governments proved to be at least as dangerous to the church as the increase in trade and the growth of urban settlements.

Efficient lay governments were dangerous to the church because they could become efficient only by obtaining a practical monopoly of political power in the districts which they controlled. Then the mere exercise of this power, even without a deliberate plan, would tend to transfer primary allegiance from the church to the state. Finally, as lay officials became aware of what was happening they could make deliberate efforts to secure the allegiance of the people. These three tendencies led to the laicization of society.

During the latter part of the twelfth and the first half of the thirteenth centuries the old mediaeval hierarchy of governments broke down in many regions. The old division of responsibility and power ended. In each region affected by these changes one government became dominant, and gained control of political activities. The dominant government was not always that of a king—in Italy, for example, it was that of the town—but whether king, count, or commune came out on top the result was the same. Only one government was left which was strong enough to inspire loyalty.

The monopoly of power secured by the dominant government was, of course, not complete. It was a *de facto* monopoly, which would not meet the tests of later political theorists any more than our present economic monopolies meet the tests of the lawyer or the economist. The political monopolies of the thirteenth century worked very much as our economic monopolies work today. Other units were tolerated, and were allowed a certain share of the business of government, as long as they recognized that they held this share only by grace of the dominant power. This is the policy of Edward I in the *Quo Warranto* proceedings, and of Philip the Fair in his *pariages* with the semi-independent feudal lords of southern France. Only admit that you hold your power from us, that you exercise it subject to our correction, and we will let you retain a large degree of jurisdiction. It was a policy which could be applied to the church fully as much as it was applied to competing lay governments. A direct attack on all ecclesiastical jurisdiction would have been futile and dangerous. Minor officials who were tactless enough to make such attacks were always disavowed by their superiors. The inner circle of royal advisers wanted to weaken the church courts, but they knew that a head-on collision of authorities

was not the best way of securing this result. They never denied that the church courts should have a certain amount of power. But they were going to define that power; ecclesiastical courts were to retain only the jurisdiction recognized by the royal council. The first example of this policy is found in the reign of Henry II of England, and while his attempt at definition was not completely successful, the precedent was not forgotten. By the end of the thirteenth century royal governments in both France and England were regularly defining the powers of church courts. The excesses of minor officials were a useful weapon in establishing this power of the central government. When the church was annoyed by such officials its only recourse was to beg the royal government to define and defend ecclesiastical jurisdictions. As Professor Graves has shown, this is the story behind *Circumspecte Agatis*[1] in England. In France, even so powerful a prelate as the bishop of Toulouse had to seek the intervention of the royal council almost every year in order to preserve the most elementary rights. The effects of this policy on public opinion are obvious. If the church's rights of government were dependent on the good will of lay rulers, if the church could maintain its jurisdiction only through the aid of the state, lay governments must be more powerful and important than the church.

Then, as certain governments obtained a *de facto* monopoly of political power they began to do more work. Their courts met more frequently, they heard more cases, they welcomed appeals from subordinate jurisdictions. These governments began to tax and to legislate, even

---

[1] A writ issued by Edward I in 1286 defining with considerable precision the jurisdiction of church courts.—Ed.

though taxation was at first considered little better than robbery and legislation was felt to be sacrilegious tinkering with the sacred and unchangeable law. In order to perform this increased amount of work they multiplied the number of their officials. All this meant that they had more contacts with the mass of the people, that they touched at some point on the life of every man. No one could be ignorant of the fact that he was subject to one of these dominant governments. No one could fail to realize that the activities of his government were important, perhaps more important that the activities of the church. This sense of the increasing importance of lay governments was not the same thing as loyalty to those governments, but the first sentiment could very easily lead to the second. Men respect what is powerful and they can easily become loyal to what they respect.

The multiplication of the number of lay officials is one of the most striking phenomena of the thirteenth century. In every country the conservatives protested again and again that there were too many officials, and in every country the number of officials went right on increasing in spite of the protests. This increase had important effects on public opinion. It was not only that officials, with their friends and families, formed a large group which would support any action of the government. More important was the fact that every official, consciously or unconsciously, was a propagandist for his government. He had to spread the government's explanation of its policies; he had to enforce decisions which showed the government's power. Many officials, especially those of lower rank who were in direct contact with the people, were openly anti-clerical. The fact that such men could brutally disregard the church's rights and still keep their positions must

have convinced many people that lay governments were going to be supreme. Finally, with the steady increase in the number of government jobs a new career was opened up for able men of all classes. The church could no longer count on securing the services of the great majority of educated and intelligent men. Many laymen who might have entered the church chose to serve the king instead. Many churchmen entered the service of lay governments and became so absorbed in that service that they forgot their duty to the church. And as the church lost exclusive control of the educated class it lost much of its ability to control public opinion.

Fully as important as the increase in the number of permanent lay officials was the increase in the number of men who were not officials, but who were forced to aid the government in its work from time to time. Professor A. B. White has shown how much of the work of local government in England was performed by juries, or selected knights of the shire. France had a much larger paid bureaucracy, but even in France the royal government could not function without requiring the services of its subjects. In France as in England, local notables were associated with royal officials in administrative investigations or judicial inquests. In France, as in England, thousands of men were forced to aid the government in the wearisome work of assessing and collecting taxes. For example, when the aid for knighting Louis of Navarre was collected in 1314, there were 322 collectors in the viscounty of Paris alone, excluding the city proper and the castellany of Poissy. It seems unlikely that many people enjoyed dropping their own work in order to spend days and weeks in serving the government for little or no pay. Yet the men who performed these expensive and burdensome tasks did not become disloyal to the government which imposed them. Rather they became increasingly conscious of the dignity and power of secular government. They acquired the habit of obedience to lay authorities, they accepted the point of view of the permanent officials with whom they had frequent contacts. A modern parallel to this process would be found in the results of military conscription. Most men who are drafted into an army regard military service as a burden. Yet compulsory military service has proved one of the most successful means for building up fanatical loyalty to the state. Just so the compulsory civil service of the thirteenth century created loyalty to the governments which imposed it.

The processes discussed so far worked indirectly, and almost automatically, to build up loyalty to lay governments. It was natural for any ruler to try to increase his power in a given area. As he gained a virtual monopoly of power it was necessary for him to add new functions to his government and to increase the number of men who assisted him in governing. There was little theorizing behind these developments, merely the desire to gain power and to use that power effectively. But the result of this drive for power was the creation of something very like a sovereign state. There was no place for such an entity in the old mediaeval system; it was absolutely opposed to the belief in the unity of Christendom and the hierarchy of political organizations. It had to be justified, explained, sold to the people. As a result, toward the end of the thirteenth century a definite theory to justify laicization appears.

This theory, like so many other things in the thirteenth century, was the work of lawyers. This new class of men, pro-

duced by the increased activity of twelfth-century governments, set the tone of the thirteenth century even more than the new class produced by increased business activity. The thirteenth century was a legalistic century, a century in which men sought exact definitions of all human relationships, a century in which men wanted to work out the logical implications of all general ideas and projects, a century in which men wanted to complete and to justify the work of their predecessors. And because the thirteenth century was legalistic, because it was a period of definitions and detailed explanations, it was a much less tolerant century than the twelfth. It was no longer possible to harmonize divergent views by thinking of them as merely different aspects of universal truth. Thus definition of the doctrines of the church forced many reformers into heresy. Definition of the rights of the state forced many men to chose between loyalty to the state and loyalty to the church. If was only when a choice had to be made that laicization was possible.

The definition of the powers of the ruler worked out by thirteenth-century lawyers developed into something which was almost a theory of the sovereign state. Such a theory could not be reconciled with the old mediaeval system; it forced a choice between loyalties. Briefly, it ran something like this. First, there are definite boundaries to all states. The twelfth century had known spheres of influence rather than boundaries; power decreased in proportion to the distance from the ruler until a region was reached in which his authority was counterbalanced by that of another lord. In the thirteenth-century theory the power of the dominant government was to extend, undiminished, to a precise frontier. This idea may be seen especially clearly in the south of France, where royal officials worked steadily to fix an exact boundary with Aragon, where they insisted again and again that the eastern boundary of the realm was the Rhone; where they flatly denied that there could be a no man's land of independent bishoprics, in which the king's authority was neutralized by that of the emperor. Then, within these precise boundaries there is to be a definite superior, who can supervise and correct the work of all subordinate governments. This idea may be found in England earlier than in France, but it was most clearly expressed by Beaumanoir:[2] "The king is sovereign over all, and has as his right the general guardianship of all the realm . . . There is none so great beneath him that he cannot be haled to his court for default of justice or for false judgment." Moreover, this definite superior, if he observes certain formalities, may issue orders which are binding on all men in the realm. As the *dictum de Kenilworth*[3] says: "The king, and his legitimate orders and instructions, must be fully obeyed by each and every man, great and small, in the realm" Guillaume de Plaisian[4] is even more emphatic: "All those in the realm are ruled by the king's authority; even prelates and clerks, in temporal matters, are bound by the laws, edicts, and constitutions of the king." The central government may state the law, or make special rulings where the laws fail to give a solution to a problem. This was recognized in England as early as Glanvill's time,[5] when it was said that laws

for the entire kingdom might be made "in doubtful cases by the authority of the prince with the advice of the magnates." It took somewhat longer for this power to be recognized in France, but by the end of the thirteenth century Beaumanoir could say: "The king may make such establishments as please him for the common good, and that which he establishes must be obeyed." For the common good taxes may be imposed on all property in the kingdom. The most extreme statement of this right was made by Guillaume de Plaisian: "Everything within the boundaries of his realm is the lord king's, at least as to protection, superior jurisdiction, and lordship. Even as property it is the king's, for he can give, receive, and use any property, movable and immovable, in his realm for the public good and defense of the kingdom." An English lawyer would not have said this, but the English government did insist that all property could be taxed for defense of the realm. Finally, while no lesser political authority can be exempt from, or control the decisions of the king, there is no higher political authority which can interfere with the king's powers of government. Here English and French lawyers are equally emphatic. Bracton's[6] "the king has no equal, much less a superior" is matched in a letter sent by the French government to the Emperor Henry VII: "Since the time of Christ the realm of France has had only its own king, who never recognized nor had a temporal superior."

These ideas add up to something very like the theory of sovereignty. Within fixed boundaries there is a definite superior who has the final decision regarding all political activities. It is not quite

---

[2] An important administrator and adviser of Louis IX of France (1226–1270) and author of the legal tract "Customs of Beauvais."—Ed.

[3] A "statute" of Henry III of England issued in 1266.—Ed.

[4] One of the influential royal lawyers of the French court in the early fourteenth century.—Ed.

[5] Ranulf de Glanville (d. 1190) was an English administrator and author of the "Treatise on the Laws and Customs of England," the first serious commentary on English law.—Ed.

---

[6] Henry de Bracton (d. 1268) was an English ecclesiastic and judge who advanced the work of Glanville in his more systematic "On the Laws and Customs of England."—Ed.

the theory of sovereignty, not only because the word is lacking, but also because it is a theory of comparative rather than absolute power. The words which the French lawyers use show this: the king has "superioritas," he has "majus dominium," he has "altior dominatio."[7] His power is greater than that of any subject, but it is not a different power; he makes the final decisions, but he does not make all the decisions. But, sovereignty or not, this theory clearly conflicts with earlier mediaeval ideas. It sets up the kingdom as the most important unit of government and demands that all subjects give their primary allegiance to the kingdom.

Moreover, these ideas were not the work of isolated theorists. Every quotation which has been given was written by a high royal official. Most of them were taken from official documents—laws, pleas in royal courts, or letters written in the king's name. Innumerable statements of a similar sort could be found in official records. This means that everyone who attended a royal court, everyone who did business with the government, was exposed to the new theories. This must have done a great deal to spread the idea of the supremacy of royal government, and hence, to make laicization easier. Even this was not enough, and at the end of the century deliberate propaganda in favor of the new theories was begun in both France and England. Local and national assemblies were called, at which royal officials could expound their new doctrine. It has long been apparent that the Estates-General and local assemblies held in France at the time of the quarrel with Boniface were called solely for purposes of propaganda. In a book recently published, Professor C. H. Taylor of Harvard has given strong reasons for

believing that the French assemblies which met to consider taxation were called primarily to create a public opinion favorable to taxation. They did not consent to taxation; in 1314, for example, the tax was already ordered before the assembly met. But they could be impressed by arguments showing the necessity for taxation, and they would report those arguments to their constituents. I feel that the same thing is true of the English Parliament, as far as the knights and burgesses were concerned. True, they were asked to assent to taxation, but their assent was, at first, a matter of form. Much more important was the fact that they could be harangued by royal officials, that they could be used to spread propaganda which would make the work of the tax-collector easier.

At the same time the governments of France and England began to encourage nationalism in order to gain support for their policies. There had always been a certain amount of latent nationalism in Europe; the French had sneered at the drunken English and the Italians had despised the boorish Germans. But this early nationalism had not been very strong in comparsion with provincial loyalties and it had been frowned on by lay and ecclesiastical rulers alike. It was contrary to the basic principles of Christianity and it was dangerous to lay rulers whose territories seldom coincided with national units and whose policies were not always nationalistic. The concentration of political authority in France and England encouraged the growth of nationalism by decreasing the differences between provinces and increasing the differences between countries. But even in the middle of the thirteenth century nationalism was not yet respectable. Nationalism was associated with rebellion against constituted authority, with such movements as the protests of the English

---

[7] "Superiority," "the higher power," "superior power."—Ed.

clergy against papal exactions, or the opposition of the English baronage to Henry III. Men like St Louis[8] and Henry III, who believed sincerely in the old international ideals, could not follow a nationalistic policy. In fact, many of Henry's troubles were caused by his unwillingness to accept the nationalistic ideas of his selfish and narrow-minded barons. About 1300, however, the governments of France and England began to see that nationalism could be useful to them, and once the idea was supported by a recognized authority it grew rapidly. At one point in the war over Gascony, Edward I, accused the French of wishing to annihilate the English race and the anti-clerical legislation of his reign shows a tacit acceptance of nationalistic ideas. In France, the government appealed even more openly to nationalism. During the struggle against Boniface VIII repeated efforts were made to convince the country that the pope was anti-French, and that he was threatening the independence of France. In the same way when the French clergy were asked for money to carry on the war with Flanders, they were reminded of the pre-eminence of France as a Christian country and were told that it was their duty as Frenchmen to defend their native land. In 1305 the king wrote to the clergy of the province of Tours: "You should realize that all the clergy and laity of our kingdom, like members of one body . . . are bound to give each other spiritual and temporal aid to preserve, defend, and protect the unity of this realm." The extremes to which French nationalism could go appear in the ingenious schemes of Pierre Dubois for subjecting all Europe to French rule. It is true that Dubois was only a minor official, and was never promoted, but

---

[8] Louis IX, king of France (1226–1270).—Ed.

that does not mean that his views were not in harmony with those of the central administration. Generally speaking, minor officials spoke more bluntly, and acted more brutally than the immediate advisers of the king, but the basic ideas of the two groups were the same. A tactless minor official, such as Dubois, might not be promoted, but neither would he be discharged. And the views of such a man, since they were never expressly repudiated, might be very influential with certain groups.

When Boniface VIII, alarmed by the growing power of lay governments, tried to limit their authority, he found that he was too late. The people of France and England remained loyal to their kings; there was not even a half-hearted rebellion in favor of the pope. In France the government had such control of public opinion that it was able to seize the church's own weapon of a charge of heresy and turn it against Boniface. A few years later it succeeded in ruining the Templars by the same method. This perhaps marks the extreme limit of mediaeval laicization —a secular ruler determines the policy of the church and uses the church for his own ends. This feat was not immediately repeated, but from the time of Boniface on there was no doubt that lay rulers had the primary allegiance of their people. Society was controlled, as far as it was controlled at all, by lay governments and not by the church. It is true that during the fourteenth and fifteenth centuries this lay control was not always very intelligent, nor very effective. During these years there was a reaction against central governments; a reaction caused, at least in part, by the fact that they had gained power by a mixture of blackmail, chicanery, and bullying and that a generation educated in these techniques began to use them against their rulers. But this very period of weak lay government showed how effective the work of laicization had been. The church could not regain its old power in spite of the opportunity afforded by a new period of anarchy. There was no substitute for centralized, lay government in France or England, however weak that government might be.

The reaction against central governments after 1300 may explain why laicization went no further; why education, and care of the sick and poor remained in the province of the church. But it should also be remembered that mediaeval governments were satisfied with relative, rather than absolute power. Totalitarianism was foreign to their ways of thinking—it would also have been too expensive. Police work cost money—so there was no objection to letting the barons do much of it. Education was expensive—so there was no objection to letting the church do it. Some townspeople in England and France did object to church control of education and tried to set up their own schools, but as far as I know the count of Flanders was the only lay ruler who gave any support to this movement. As for social service work, the whole tendency was to make the church do more of it, rather than less. Anyone who has studied grants to the church must have been struck by the great increase in the number of gifts made specifically to hospitals, poor-houses, and university colleges after the middle of the thirteenth century. The old unlimited grant for the general purposes of the church almost disappears in the fourteenth century. This may be, indirectly, a form of laicization; the church is to be made to do "useful" work instead of spending its money on purely religious purposes. But there is no hesitation in allowing the church to perform these services; rather it is encouraged to do so. Not until the next great wave of laicization in the sixteenth century is there an attempt to deprive the church of its educational and philanthropic functions. Once the leadership, the "superiority" of mediaeval lay governments was recognized, they had no further quarrel with the church.

In the present selection BOYD C. SHAFER (b. 1907) surveys the development of national feeling from the twelfth to the eighteenth centuries and takes a position somewhere between the extremes of Kohn and Huizinga. In his opinion there are definite connections between some of the ideas and institutions of the later Middle Ages and modern nationalism. Nonetheless, he warns us to avoid thinking of these medieval manifestations as "the thing itself," and argues that they are only precursors of the sentiment we can properly call nationalism. Given the differences among the preceding authors, how is the student to judge when something ceases to be a precursor and becomes "the thing itself"?*

Boyd C. Shafer

The Early Development of Nationality

To write a full history of nationalism would be to write a multivolumed history of the Western world since the twelfth century and the history of the rest of the world for at least the last hundred years. This chapter attempts only to survey the origin of basic historical forces and ideas which contributed, often later as they developed in another context, to the rise of nationalism in western Europe and the United States from roughly the twelfth to the eighteenth century.

Beyond the vast mass of material which had to be examined, three major difficulties arose. Often students of nationalism . . . have tried to find simple explanations for the rise of national feeling and have employed "either-or" instead of the conjunction "and." The present writer would be happy to find an explanation, a single hypothesis which would definitively explain why and how nationalism arose. But the reasons for nationalism are many, complex, and intertwined. The difficulty is not to find the *one* explanation; rather it is to be certain that many are examined. The writer is under no illusion that this difficulty has here been entirely overcome. Secondly, since the factors which have led to nationalism cannot be resurrected, they cannot be isolated, and their causal validity cannot be tested. Those described here are those which in our present state of knowledge and climate of opinion seem to have contributed most. The historian can only

---

present what he hopes are the best guesses on the basis of the evidence the past has left us. Thirdly, historians and patriots often have tended to see forces which later might develop into nationalism as the thing itself, or to see a direct line of development from certain possible origins to the full flowering of the ideas when such development may not have occurred. To avoid this kind of erroneous thinking is not easy. But the evidence seems to tell us that modern nationalism developed slowly and became evident in the full sense only with the eighteenth century and the French Revolution. When, therefore, this chapter goes back into the late medieval period, this does not mean that nationalism is to be found there but only that certain institutions and ideas then arose or existed which *later* became part of modern concepts of nation and nationalism.

Sentiments akin to nationalism are possibly as old and as prevalent as man and society. Each people, from primitive tribe to modern nation, seems to regard itself as the center of the world, as somehow distinct, as "real men," and each seems to have evidenced some kind of group feeling. Some men, especially the more primitive ones, have been intensely loyal to a tribe. Some have, as in fifth-century B.C. Athens and Sparta, been united by a common devotion to a city-state. Some have looked up to and jointly served an emperor like the Roman Augustus or the sixteenth-century Charles V. Some, in ancient Israel or medieval western Europe, have possessed a common faith in a creed or in a religious leader. Some have held it an honor or duty to be a member of a feudal class as in tenth-century France. Because of loyalty or compulsion, some have followed an absolute king such as Louis XIV. Some have lived and fought unitedly, as in Nazi Germany, because of a belief in a master race. Some, the Marxian communists, for example, have believed themselves bound together as a class by inexorable material law. Men have been, then, united by belief in or loyalty to tribe, city-state, emperor, creed, feudal class, monarchy, race, and economic law.

These loyalties are chiefly to be distinguished from modern nationalism by the object of the loyalty. In some of the ancient Greek states the patriotic devotion of the citizens (not the slaves or other inhabitants) to their city, possibly cannot be distinguished in any other way. They are also different because today not just some but nearly *all* men are principally and most significantly united and divided by their devotion to only *one* object, their own nation.

The nation as institution and symbol, it must be emphasized, has meant different things; conceptions have varied with time, place, and the individual. Usually, however, the word refers to (1) a definite state which in early modern times was dynastic and in modern times has been democratic or dictatorial, (2) a definite territory though it has varied in size and seldom has been considered large enough, and (3) a group of people who possess a distinctive common culture— language, literature, history, and a common hope to live together in the future. The major problem here is to determine how, for our own time, the common state, territory, and culture became established and how men became devoted to them, that is, loyal to the nation.

Historically it is possible to trace the origins of modern nations at least to the break-up of Charlemagne's empire when western Europe was roughly split into Latin and Germanic sections. But neither well-developed nations nor widespread national feeling can be said to exist for hundreds of years thereafter. As Professor Joseph Strayer has observed, "The scale of allegiance [during the Middle Ages] of most men would have gone something like this: I am first of all a Christian, second a Burgundian, and only third a Frenchman." A few of the Western nations, particularly England and France, began to emerge into some definite form beyond the local feudal state or domain before the end of the twelfth century, and national consciousness arose still later. No definite dates, of course, can be set; both the extension of government and territory and the realization of a common culture necessary for the creation of the nation were slow, occurring over a long period of time. Nation building began without planning or design, and usually proceeded that way; it was not a continuous but an intermittent and sporadic process; and it still goes on.

While the forces which early built the nation cannot be precisely isolated and evaluated, the royal dynasties which were at first but strong feudal families were of major significance. If René Johannet, the French historian of nationalism, exaggerated, he was partly right when he wrote, "The cause of the statue is not the marble but the artist. In the case of nationality, it is primarily the dynasty." In France and England as well as later in Spain, Germany, Italy, and Russia, the strongest and perhaps luckiest noble families won the territory and, with their supporters, created the monarchical governments which became national.

At the beginning and through their history these families primarily desired territory, wealth, prestige, and power. They did not think that they were creating nations and certainly during their early years little national feeling existed anywhere in their domains. In France especially, and in England usually, the chief feudal lord, the king, simply tried to enlarge his own domain and his own feudal power. The first he accomplished through war and conquest, diplomacy and duplicity, marriage and purchase, inheritance, legal and illegal confiscation of feudal vassals' property, and perhaps through fortuitous circumstance. The second he gained through the provision of royal laws, the levying of royal taxes, the creation of an official class (especially lawyers) dependent upon the monarchy, and the general substitution, whenever possible, of royal authority for what had been the rule of lesser and more local feudal princes or for the claims of the universal Church. . . .

The role of the dynasties in building the territorial foundations of other nations may not have been as obvious nor as decisive as it was in France. In England, however, and later in Russia, Germany, and Italy, royal families played vital although differing roles as they sought to enlarge their personal domains. In every case it was not so much the extension of national "royal" power as the enlargement of the king's personal domain which created the territorial basis for the nation. The kings were seldom nationalistic in any modern sense.

So important was dynastic striving for territory in the early history of nation building that it would be easy to overstress it and ignore other forces of equal importance. As the dynasties extended their domains they usually also built personal governmental agencies, executive, legislative, judicial, and administrative institutions. These *later* would become the national agencies and institutions. Sometimes, it is true, national political institutions were beginning to grow, partly in opposition to the royal power, as in the case of the English Parliament. But in France and England early, and in Russia, Germany, and Italy later, the monarchical state tended to shape the society and attempted with great success to centralize and to unify and thus to make the society over into a unit that was powerful and could be conveniently governed and led. Here again, as in the case of territory, the monarchs were seeking not national but personal power and glory. Often they would have preferred to be building a personal empire like that of the Hapsburgs and Charles V in the sixteenth century. Perhaps it is to be regretted in the light of subsequent events that geographic space, poor communication, and intense personal rivalries prevented one ruler for all of Europe. As events happened, no one ruler could become strong enough, and any one monarch who so threatened immediately became the object of attack by the others. The result was not one empire but a series of independent monarchical and later national states.

The chief object of the monarchs was to enlarge their domain and intensify their sway over it. It was to build a state, a dynastic state for the purpose of furthering the power and glory of the prince. It was primarily *étatism*,[1] not nationalism, which characterized the governments of the Bourbons and Tudors and most other dynasties. If the national interests were considered, they were regarded as synonymous with those of the monarch. While no kings ever said, *"La nation, c'est moi"* ["I am the nation"—Ed.], they often so thought and acted. And when they did they were establishing the governmental as well as the territorial foundation of the modern nation. In order to gain and retain power they had to create central

governmental agencies. They had to obtain money through centrally levied and collected taxes, to establish a royal army and navy, and to erect a superior court system. And to carry out their will and government they had to have a great number of loyal royal officials. While the taxes, armed forces, courts, and officials were not national at first, they would become increasingly so. Without conscious design, then, the nation-state was coming into being.

Again, these developments took place in different ways at different times in different countries. In early Norman England, but not in the France of the same period, all vassals were directly responsible to the king, and, except in border lands, did not possess the rights to administer high justice, coin money, or wage private war. Later in England the nobility and upper middle class shared the royal power more than in most countries, while in France the monarchy, with its allies from the middle classes, played a more significant role, the aristocracy usually opposing centralizing tendencies. So far as the nation-state was concerned, the result was much the same. As the royal central government became more extensive and powerful, the governmental bases of the nation were being laid down.

In England the kings from the Norman William the Conqueror (1066–1087) to the Stuart James I (1603–1625), though they at times were forced to share their power with a parliament representative of the upper classes, used their ancient feudal rights as well as their military might to strengthen the central government. William the Conqueror, treating England as a feudal property, forced all fief holders to swear allegiance directly to him. He collected the facts for the old Danegeld tax in a survey so closely made "that there was not one single hide nor rood of land

---

[1] "Statism," here used as a synonym for "royalism" or "dynasticism"—Ed.

nor . . . was there an ox, cow or swine that was not set down in the writ." Henry II (1154–1189), though no trueborn Englishman, made possible the continued growth of English common law by enlarging the power and scope of the royal courts from the *royal curia* on down, thus reducing those of the local, feudal, and church courts. He began the practices of regularly using juries and of sending down itinerant justices to enforce the royal laws, and their decisions were a significant source of the developing common or universal law of the realm. While his judges were as much interested in collecting royal revenue as in enforcing justice, the royal central government was strengthened in either case. In pressing need of revenue he succeeded in levying royal taxes upon all personal property and incomes. And in his Assize of Arms of 1181 he commanded what weapons all Englishmen should possess for the royal service, thus reducing the power of the nobility and enhancing his own. Henry II thus "left England with a judicial and administrative system and a habit of obedience to government." Henry III (1216–1272) continued to send down royal commissioners, the "General Eyre," to examine the financial and judicial business of the shire officials. In order to get taxes for his war with Philip IV of France and expand his own royal power, Edward I (1272–1307) called what was later termed the "Model Parliament," and this Parliament was the prototype of the body which much later became the chief agency of the British national government and took the place of the monarch in unifying Britain. Under Edward also began the English Statute Law which, among other things, restated and more precisely defined the feudal real property laws and made them uniformly applicable to the whole kingdom. Edward III (1327–1377) appointed justices of the peace to interpret royal law and justice in every county; these royally appointed officials by Elizabeth's time concerned themselves with nearly all local legal matters from petty offenses to the building of roads and the enforcement of the poor law.

By the close of the medieval period the English monarchy had strengthened the central government, established national institutions, begun English national law, and created a class of governmental lawyers and officials who were always interested in protecting and advancing the interests of the royal nation-state. More important here, it had taught the English people to look to the central government rather than to lord or priest for protection and security. If the "King's Peace" was indifferently enforced, it was better than any the lesser feudal lords could offer. Hence, under royal aegis the nation-state in England was well on its way to acquiring unlimited sovereignty. Even when opposition to the monarchy's absolute power arose as in the reigns of John (1199–1216) and Henry II, when English constitutional government may be said to have its beginnings, the result was to stimulate interest on the part of the nobility and burgesses in the central government, a government that was primarily royal but that could become national.

The distinguished British medievalist, VIVIAN H.
GALBRAITH (b. 1889), is professor of history in Oriel
College, Oxford University. Best known for his studies
of English chronicles and chroniclers, he here brings
his vast knowledge of those subjects to bear upon the
problem of nationalism. In his own words the present
article represents "the core" of his teaching on the
relationship between language and nationality in
medieval English history.*

Vivian H. Galbraith

Language and Nationality

A nation may be defined as any considerable group of people who believe they *are* one; and their nationalism as the state of mind which sustains this belief. Broadly speaking, the sentiment of nationality is much the same in quality at all times and in all places. Its minimum content is love, or at least awareness, of one's country, and pride in its past achievements, real or fictitious; and it springs from attachment to the known and familiar, stimulated by the perception of difference—difference of habits and customs, often too of speech, from those of neighbouring peoples. The historical evidence for the existence of this positive sentiment in early times is largely inferential, a mere deduction from the struggles and mutual hatreds of tribes perpetually at war. But by the tenth or eleventh century there is evidence that medieval man was faintly stirred by the same sort of national impulses as we are, though he felt them in very different circumstances, in a different degree and, often, in relation to other objects. By the thirteenth century the fully developed medieval state had reached a momentary equilibrium, and if it was still "feudal," it was also, in its way, a national state. Then as now, nationality was in general, though not necessarily, coterminous with a vernacular. But it was moulded and defined by a universal Latin culture, and its history chiefly recorded

*From Vivian H. Galbraith, "Nationality and Language in Medieval England," *Transactions of the Royal Historical Society*, XXIII (1941), 113–129. Reprinted by permission of the Society and Professor Galbraith. Footnotes omitted.

in Latin chronicles. The vernaculars played a subordinate *role* and if, in England for example, we study medieval nationalism only in vernacular poetry and homilies, the Ormulum, the Ancren Riwle and English or French chronicles, we shall miss much of its character and achievement. There was not yet that close, emotional association of national feeling with the vernacular (it is here contended) that distinguishes contemporary nationality. The beginnings of this connexion lie in the fourteenth and fifteenth centuries, when the medieval state was past its best.

The real nationalities of the early Middle Age were much smaller than those of to-day. If we imagine a medieval man saying, "My country, right or wrong," he would be referring to Normandy, Mercia, Bavaria, even to Pisa or Florence, rather than to France, England, Germany, or Italy. The primary groupings of the Middle Ages were, in fact, the provincial or regional nationalities. These were first hammered into shape by powerful princes and then gradually swallowed up in the larger modern units. The main outlines of potentially greater nationalities are nevertheless discernible from a very early period, for they rest upon the solid foundations of tribal grouping and language. Franks, Germans, and Englishmen are well distinguished before the tenth century and had arrived at some sort of external unity in their political organisation. In England where the situation was complicated by the Scandinavian occupation of the north-east in the late ninth century and the Norman conquest in the eleventh, the simultaneous working of nationality on both planes is clearly traceable. The Danish conquest superimposed on the original provincial

nationalities a division of the country into two nations, yet without destroying its formal unity: and a century later it was still an open question which would prevail. The foreign sympathies of Edward the Confessor[1] and the Norman conquest excited a common "English" hatred of the conquerors, which perhaps transcended, though it hardly differed in kind from, the regional antipathies of north and south, of Dane and West Saxon. The feudal order was indeed compatible with both types of "national" sentiment. All political relations were then personal relations, and the personal tie which (generally through the tenure of land) joined every man to some other above him in the social hierarchy, ultimately connected the serf with the king of the Franks, the king of the English or even with the Roman Emperor himself. The French monarchy, for example, was thus preserved through the tenth and eleventh centuries, when France was in fact divided into a dozen or more virtually independent states, provincial nationalities, whose rulers governed their lands and ordered their policy with complete freedom.

The feudal tie—the personal devotion of a man to his lord—was in short the moving force of medieval society and determined political development at both levels. For in the first place, it settled feudal geography. The effective national unit was a region small enough for the prince to know personally and to control all his immediate vassals, and the more important medial tenants. Flanders, Normandy, Anjou are typical examples, while in post-Conquest England central control was just, but only just, maintained. To realise that England had reached the

---

[1] King of England, 1042–1066.—Ed.

geographical limit we need only examine the Norman attempts to absorb Wales, Scotland, and Ireland. Secondly, the feudal tie strictly limited the possibilities of centralisation. The feudal prince, it is often said, was and remained throughout the Middle Ages only *primus inter pares,* the first in an aristocratic society of social equals. This, of course, is not the whole truth, though it is a rough approximation to the facts. The prince was always, and increasingly, something more than feudal. The Church, for example, invested him with peculiar prerogatives incompatible with this definition; and it is the strength of the Middle Ages that contradictory assertions rarely prevented a working compromise. But the fact remains that while there is a great deal of royal centralisation at the expense of the third estate, the franchises of the nobles remained as legitimate and "divine," and therefore as unsusceptible of legal limitation as those of the king himself. Royal power differed more in degree than in kind from that of the great vassals, and their liberties (in England) only ended with their destruction in the fifteenth century.

Thus personal lordship cut across, and in some ways blunted the edge of nationalism, especially the larger nationalism, in the Middle Ages. There were, too, other limiting forces: the universal Church, for example, even though, for its own purposes, at times it fostered national differences; the uncentralised, unachieved character of the medieval state; the slower pulse of political life in an overwhelmingly agricultural society; the conflicting claims of corporate separateness in civic and economic life; the class divisions, often bitter; and finally, the dazzling prestige of the Latin tongue which retarded the acceptance of the vernaculars. For these and other reasons, national feeling was only one of several competing forces towards social coherence. To-day nearly all these limitations have disappeared, leaving free play to the all-pervading rabid nationalism of contemporary Europe. The restricted nationalism of the Middle Ages is further illustrated by the poverty of medieval Latin, which had but the single word *natio* to describe the Slavs, the English, the Saxons, or the Florentines. With the growth of the idea comes, by abstraction and refinement, a wider vocabulary. The word "nation" is found in the fourteenth century with something of a modern sense; and "national" in the sixteenth. "Nationally" and "nationality" appear in the seventeenth: "nationalise" in the eighteenth: and "nationalism" and "nationalisation" only in the nineteenth. To these we must add a mass of poetic metaphor and personification in which the literary expression of the more recent mass sentiment is encrusted—the Flag, the Fatherland, "My England," and so on. Nationalism, which to-day is as much the province of the poet as the politician, might even at first sight appear to be different in kind from the medieval sentiment; but it would be unwise to deny it a sentimental or emotional force before we find either an exact vocabulary or literary expression of the idea. The single term *natio,* at once more concrete and more general than its derivatives, may hide a hundred shades of meaning, and the difference between the medieval and the modern feeling of nationality be no more than one of degree.

The sentiment of nationality is thus a continuous thread in the stuff of English history, present in some primitive form from the beginning, but in the Middle Ages still relatively inconspicuous.

Historians are wont to measure its growth and intensification by the progress of the vernacular, which, as is well known, developed in a unique and precocious way in the tenth and eleventh centuries. By the year 1000 we meet with a formed, literary English prose, and very little later, an "official English" used by the central government. Professor Chambers, who, in a brilliant essay has recently brought together the indications of a national feeling in England at this time, lays great stress on this prose, and in particular on the fact that it is such good prose. He says, in effect, that there are few better tests of a people having reached and maintained its place among nations than the power of writing stirring prose in its own tongue: that from some points of view it seems as if eleventh-century England was getting into the fifteenth without passing through the later Middle Ages at all: and that the English language and English nationality were both nearly destroyed by the Norman Conquest. There can of course be no doubt about the existence of some sort of a national consciousness in pre-Conquest England. Behind the official English lies a century of more or less continuous political pressure exerted by a line of energetic kings which certainly did something to beat England into political unity; and the emergence of a homiletic, literary prose was undoubtedly an educative influence, in politics as well as in religion, upon lay society. But we must be careful not to read back the present into the past by assuming that the vernacular was as important an element in national feeling then as it is now. For if we make this mistake we shall greatly exaggerate the strength of Saxon national feeling, and what is worse, we shall miss the fact that it was a continuous sentiment which, surviving the Norman Conquest, brings us after three centuries of expansion to the more-national England of the fifteenth century.

The point is not so much whether *we* admire the prose of the Anglo-Saxons and think it good, as whether *they* thought it good and took pride in it as a literary language. Actually there is little evidence of any such attitude. The vernacular in England as elsewhere was a second best, and its diffusion a sign of national illiteracy. It was encouraged by Alfred[2] because of the dearth of Latin scholarship, and used by Aelfric,[3] very reluctantly, to carry the message of salvation to the laity. The early vernacular poetry, it may be, embodies many a glimmer of still less than half-realised national feeling, but the early prose is due to the practical necessity of saving souls or governing people in a land that lacked an adequate supply of Latin-writing men. It could hardly be otherwise in an age when learning and Latin were virtually synonymous. Latin was the language of the clergy; the only learned language; the only language studied grammatically; the only language that could adequately express the thoughts of sophisticated men on letters, religion, science, and mathematics. It was, in short, the language of Rome in a still backward-looking civilisation. True, it had been a dead language for at least three centuries (else had the vernaculars never arisen): yet it could be and was spoken as Esperanto and Ido are spoken, while for literature, learning, and business its credit was not anywhere to be seriously challenged before the thirteenth century. From start to finish, Latin was the reluctant foster-mother of the vernaculars all over Europe. It was learned clerks

---

[2] King of England, 871–899.—Ed.

[3] Abbot of Eynsham (fl. 1000) who translated Latin into Anglo-Saxon for the benefit of "unschooled" laymen.—Ed.

who gave the Roman alphabet to the various local *patois,* and (chiefly by translation from Latin) slowly raised them to the literary level. Practical necessity applied this process first and most intensely in England. Soon English was caught up and overtaken, first by French and then by Italian. These in turn reacted upon English, and so, indirectly, prolonged and extended the influence of Latin upon the vernacular. In such a world as this, to equate nationality with the literary achievements of the vernacular, to the exclusion of Latin culture, is to ignore the realities of medieval national life.

There is little to show that in pre-Conquest England national feeling, which was real enough, was as yet bound up with an emotional affection for the vernacular either in literature or in public life. The coming together of nationality and language was scarcely, in fact, to begin for more than two centuries. Nor is this surprising. The national feeling of the eleventh, twelfth, and thirteenth centuries, though steadily widening, was inevitably feudal and aristocratic. Then, as now, it centred on the person of the ruler, but an intelligent grasp of royal policy (not to speak of actual participation in it) was confined to the few. The social and educational gap between the noble and the peasant counted for more than the bond of a common tongue, and more forceful ties were found in their joint interest in the land and their common loyalty to the king. The rustic's England was hardly larger than his native Hundred, and his politics reached no further than the local manor house. Yet he was knit and woven into the body politic just because the life of the manor-community was so intensely local. It is, I think, a modern anachronism to imagine in the twelfth century an "English" nation under the heel of a foreign dynasty and

its foreign barons. A *risorgimento* is precisely what we do *not* find in twelfth-century England or later. On the contrary, that the English very quickly transferred their loyalty to the Norman dynasty, is well attested. It took rather longer to reconcile them to the new nobility, but this was probably accomplished within a century. In the twelfth century, just because it was an aristocratic age, foreign conquest carried with it no proscription of local ways of life and no deliberate assimilation. From the first day of his reign, William duke of the Normans ruled in England as king of the English, making no more deliberate changes than necessity demanded. And so, while the military system was at once revolutionised, the old chancery, the old finance, the old law courts and the old laws persisted. What was true of the king, was true *mutatis mutandis* of his barons. Freeman[4] long ago pointed out that no effort was made to "strangle" the English tongue. Latin supplanted English as the literary and official medium, we cannot doubt, with general approval, and French, too, rather later, won on its merits. William of Malmesbury[5] in a famous passage contrasts the vanished English nobility with their Norman conquerors, but without reference to their vernacular. It is only, in fact, at the very end of the thirteenth century, that we first find the vernacular associated with patriotism, and still another century before we meet with the suggestion that the Normans deliberately suppressed the English language. We are forced to accept the fact (however repugnant to modern feeling) that the English after no great interval gave the old loyalty to the new and

---

[4] Edward A. Freeman, a nineteenth-century British historian best known for his multivolume *History of the Norman Conquest.* — Ed.

[5] A twelfth-century English chronicler. — Ed.

homogeneous Norman ruling class. The Normans in their turn had Edward the Confessor added to the list of saints, and quickly identified themselves with the romantic national history purveyed in Geoffrey of Monmouth's *Historia regum Britanniae* ["The History of the Kings of Britain"—Ed.], the source of the medieval Brut chronicle. Henceforth this is the popular expression of medieval national feeling; and it filtered down through countless translations and adaptations in French and English to an ever-growing audience of illiterate readers. Already in the reign of Henry II, by a development that was substantially continuous, England was in every significant sense of the term, more of a nation than in 1065.

The fact is apparent in the contemporary literature. Nationality, like all the governing ideas of the Middle Age, was seen through the eyes of Latin ecclesiastics, and received its literary expression from men whose first assumption was a sovereign Church which from the ninth to the thirteenth century became in theory and practice more universal, more Roman. This was, indeed, the true line of advance and of education in that age. It is not therefore really paradoxical that the proper source for the study of medieval national feeling in the twelfth century is the works of the Latin historians. They show how quickly the clerk, whose loyalty was to the land and its past (especially through the saints and the privileges of his church) was developing a local, English allegiance. William of Malmesbury, for example, breathes nationality, and in excellent Latin. His very grasp of English history—so far in advance of anything seen for centuries—marks a step forward in national consciousness, and a very slight study of

the *Gesta Pontificum*[6] reveals an historical interest rooted in English soil. The same is true of his lesser contemporaries, such as Serlo, whose poem on the Battle of the Standard[7] is entirely English in spirit. The stubborn and illiterate warrior class, whose history and privileges alike began in 1066, held out rather longer. The sudden substitution of a new nobility for the English thegns suggested to contemporaries as well as to later writers that English nationality had perished in the Conquest; more especially as the Normans, though adaptable and tolerant, were long mindful of their common kinship, however widely they were scattered. "It was taken for granted," writes Miss Jamison,[8] "that any (Norman) family might have a relative settled in the Sicilian kingdom just as a girl to-day might speak casually of an uncle in India or a sister at the Cape." As late as the Battle of the Standard (1138) Ailred of Rivaulx puts into the mouth of Walter Espec a speech in which there is no mention of the English but only of the Normans: "Certe patres nostri et nos hanc insulam . . . in brevi nostris subdidimus legibus, nostris obsequiis mancipavimus . . . Quis Apuliam, Siciliam, Calabriam, nisi vester Normannus edomuit?" ["Certainly our fathers and we subjected this island to our laws in a short time and by our tolerance bound it to us. Who but your Normans conquered Apulia, Sicily, and Calabria?"—Ed.] But where the Church led, the nobles followed, and by the time of Henry II they too were indistinguishable from the English.

[6] This work is often cited *Gesta Pontificum Anglorum*, "Deeds of the English Bishops."—Ed.

[7] A battle between the English and Scots in 1138. —Ed.

[8] Evelyn Jamison, a twentieth-century British historian who has written on medieval Italian and Sicilian history.—Ed.

That national feeling and the vernacular had not yet come together is clearer still in the thirteenth century. The chroniclers, drawing inspiration from the past, trace to its medieval climax the history of that extensive rather than intensive nationalism which from the time of Athelstan[9] to Edward I is more the pursuit of empires than of natural boundaries. In the second half of the century the increase of some sort of political unity and the strengthening of the national conciousness are plain matters of fact. Yet all this took place at a time when England enjoyed three literary languages and three competing cultures; and (unless we throw over our Stubbs)[10] the process of amalgamation is still continuous. The country was loyal, patriotic, anti-Welsh, anti-Scottish, anti-French. It showed in fact all the essentials of national feeling, except that, so far as education allowed, it preferred Latin to French, and French to English. This is particularly true of the spoken vernacular, in regard to which England is admittedly exceptional. Robert of Gloucester, writing towards the end of the century, complains that there is no land "that holdeth not to its own speech save England only." But the exception is one that proves the rule, since, of all European states, England was then the most highly developed national unit. The use of the mother tongue was not yet a criterion of national feeling.

It was only in the fourteenth century that Europe began to be "vernacular-conscious." The change marks a clear stage in western development, and the beginning of an influence which, all over Europe, was to transform and intensify the national sentiment. Already there was everywhere pride based on national achievement. This was now followed by the appearance of a great, though not yet a national vernacular literature, based not on utility or necessity but on conscious choice. The great name is, of course, that of Dante, whose analogue in England, two generations later, is Chaucer. Both were foreign in the matter of their vernacular writings: they were, in fact, what we should call "precursors," alive to influences whose full realisation lay far ahead. For their successors, the vernacular came to have a symbolic, national value though the Middle Ages were still Latin-bound and the Renaissance was to intervene between them and the coming of the modern, vernacular, national literatures. Yet in the confused period of the fifteenth century there was progress in that direction. In England, for example, nationality and the vernacular come consciously and undeniably, if only momentarily, together for the first time in the reign of Henry V, whose despatches from France to the City of London were written, and so to speak, deliberately written in English.

The vernacular movement appeared later in England than in France and Italy, partly because a wider gap had to be bridged between the vernacular and Latin, partly because of peculiar historical difficulties connected with the existence of two vernaculars after the Norman Conquest. The genius of Chaucer pointed the way to salvation, but the language had almost to be remade under the intensive influence of French and Italian. By the sixteenth century Chaucer's syntax was as obsolete as that of his models. Only in the reign of Elizabeth do we get, as it were, a perfect correspon-

---

[9] King of England, 925–939. — Ed.

[10] William Stubbs (1825–1901) whose *Constitutional History of England* was long considered the "standard" account of medieval English governmental institutions. — Ed.

dence—an ardent, recognisable, national feeling:

This happy breed of men, this little world,
This precious stone set in the silver sea,
Which serves it in the office of a wall,
Or as a moat defensive to a house,
Against the envy of less happier lands,
This blessed spot, this earth, this realm, this
    England,

and a final discard of Latin and French in favour of a native literature:

I love Rome, but London better. I favor Italie but England more. I honor the Latin, but I worship the English.

Mulcaster's[11] enthusiasm bore fruit in his pupil Spenser, who consciously set himself to create a national, English literature comparable with that of France and Italy. From the sixteenth century onwards, the national language has never ceased to be a strong and conscious factor in the national sentiment: and since the French Revolution the association of the two has often reached the level of passionate feeling.

The very intimate association of national feeling and affection for the vernacular in the modern world must not blind us to the fact that the connexion is comparatively recent. They converge only when the natural and fashionable medium of literature is by deliberate choice discarded for "the mother tongue." For Dante the choice lay between Latin and Italian, and in the *Convivio* ["Banquet"—Ed.] he seeks to justify his choice of the vernacular in the teeth of learned prejudice and of tradition. His example is all the more striking since no man felt so strongly the claims of Latin as the sovereign literary tongue, the only "Grammar."

------

[11] Richard Mulcaster, a sixteenth-century educator who argued that English should be a part of a university curriculum.—Ed.

The relation of Latin to the vernacular is also discussed by Dante in the *De vulgari eloquentia* [*On Eloquence in the Vulgar Tongue*—Ed.]; and it was probably because he was so conscious of their conflicting claims, that his statements are not completely consistent with one another. But two things, at least, are clear. First that he considered Latin the better language, that is, the more efficient vehicle of thought. And secondly, that the vernacular "which we acquire without any rule by imitating our nurses" is "nearest to a man, inasmuch as it is most closely united to him, for it is singly and alone in his mind before any other." To say this, was to discover that Latin, however much or little it was spoken, was and had been a dead language for centuries, since it was the *materna lingua* of no one. Moved by something stronger than reason, prejudice, and literary tradition, he threw in his lot with the still unmade vernacular. It might be supposed, since Dante was still useful as a model for Ariosto a hundred and fifty years later, that his decision was, perhaps unconsciously, governed by the fact that Italian had already reached a certain fixity of development. More probably it reflects a growing awareness of, and affection for the vernacular, now becoming general throughout western Europe. In the same way we may guess that Chaucer was impelled by something new and something more than conscious choice in using English as his literary medium.

In the last resort, the meaning of nationality in the Middle Ages, turns largely upon our definition of the terms we use. The medieval state is properly defined as "feudal," so long as we do not thereby exclude the elements at least of national sentiment: or we may just as well call it "national" (as Stubbs did), so long as we recognise the existence of other and often contrary influences. Whichever course we pursue, the real difficulty is to avoid reading the present into the past. The danger is greatest for those who, rightly conscious of a national sentiment in early times, look for supporting evidence in the growth of the vernacular tongues. The affection we all feel for the mother tongue to-day, we owe ultimately to the literary achievement of pioneers, who at a fairly definite stage in European history, abandoning Latin, set themselves to make new literatures in their mother tongues. The phenomenon is more probably due to a general change in European thought and feeling than to circumstances peculiar to any one nation, such as the state of the language or the accidents of political and social unity. The change, moreover, is hardly perceptible before the fourteenth century, a truth easily and concretely grasped if we compare the Norman Conquest with the attempted conquest of Scotland by the Edwards.

> A! fredom is a noble thing
> Fredom mais man to haf liking
> Fredom all solace to man giffis
> He lifis at es that frely lifis.

Whatever the causes, the close modern association of national feeling with the vernacular began with the literary masters —like Barbour[12]—and has by their genius been gradually spread, with growing education, throughout society.

---

[12] John Barbour, a fourteenth-century Scottish poet.—Ed.

The role of war as a unifying force and thus a basic factor in the development of medieval national feeling has often been ignored by historians. In this essay FREDERICK HERTZ (1878–1956), Austrian economist and sociologist, and holder of a chair in political economy at Halle University, discusses the importance of warfare in shaping the ideas of medieval men on the subject of nationality.*

Frederick Hertz

War and the Formation
of National Traditions

The modern large nations have been mainly formed by wars partly by conquest, partly by fusion under the menace of conquest. Every nation, furthermore, has developed its personality in great wars and everywhere the national ideology and character have been deeply influenced by them. Territory and language, religion and civilization, ideas of national interest and honour, the organization of the State and the structure of society were always to a large extent the product of wars.

A war against external enemies has at all times been regarded by powerful classes as the best remedy against internal strife. Countless wars, indeed, have been waged in order to suppress or avoid the danger of internal disintegration, or in order to weld different elements into a larger national unit by evoking a common hatred and common pride. War, therefore, could be called the greatest instrument of national unification but for the fact that it also fosters the growth of forces which often imply a new menace to national unity. A typical instance was the Hundred Years War between England and France. It has decisively furthered national unity on both sides, and also developed fundamental national traditions. Later on, however, the English knights and soldiers who returned from the war had a large share in the peasants' revolt and the internal Wars of the Roses. In both countries it required the strong

*From Frederick Hertz, *Nationality in History and Politics* (New York: Humanities Press, Inc., 1944), pp. 217–223. Reprinted by permission of Routledge & Kegan Paul Ltd., London, and Humanities Press, Inc., New York. Footnotes omitted.

hand of a powerful royalty to restore unity and peace.

Great wars in which vital interests of the country are at stake usually lead to the concentration of power in the hands of the rulers and to the predominance of the military over the civil element. The consequence is a restriction of freedom, especially freedom of speech, the demand for blind obedience and the rise of a dictatorial rule. On the other hand, great wars also compel the Governments to appeal to the help of wider circles, or even to the people as a whole, and this tends to lead to an increase in popular rights and social equality. Wars therefore imply both a democratic and an anti-democratic tendency.

In many countries war has to a great extent moulded the mentality of the ruling and politically active classes who represented the nation and determined its destiny. The most important difference between English and continental conditions was that the English nobility much earlier and to a greater degree ceased to be a privileged warrior caste. Anglo-Saxon feudalism already showed a less warlike character than feudalism in the Frankish Empire. The Normans conquered England largely through their superior military organization and many maintained their warrior spirit for centuries. On the other hand, they seem also to have brought traditions with them which helped the kings to lay the foundations of the modern State. The kings revived the old national militia and promoted the demilitarization of the nobles by the prohibition of feuds and fortified castles, and by converting feudal services into contributions of money which they used for hiring mercenaries. The nobles, however, were always apprehensive of the danger which a strong royal army would imply to their power and for this reason tried to prevent its development, and especially opposed the employment of foreign mercenaries. Many of the English nobility seem soon to have had more interest in the management of their estates and in politics than in war. The knighthood of England took less part in the Crusades than that of France and Germany. Edward I gave a great impetus to the rise of national sentiment both by his organization of a representative Parliament and by his great wars of conquest in which a new military technique was used. Edward III continued both lines of policy with astonishing success. Petrarca wrote in his letters: "When I was young the English were considered the most timid of the barbarians and now they have defeated the most warlike French." This remark shows that the English before the French wars were regarded as a comparatively non-military people. They waged the French wars not with a feudal army as did the French, but with troops recruited from all ranks. In later English history factors gained considerable force which in the long run tended to discourage militarism, namely, Parliament, the commercial interests and the Christian and liberal spirit. Parliament has sometimes been more warlike than the king, but on the whole it was strongly opposed to the formation of a big army because it saw in this a possible danger to its predominance.

In France and Germany the nobility preserved their character as a warrior caste much more than was the case in England. In both countries the warlike spirit was maintained not merely by great wars against foreign enemies but also through incessant internal wars and feuds. Many attempts to restrict the feuds were made by the Church and the kings but for a long time with little success. In Germany the breakdown of the imperial power in

Italy after the death of Frederick II and its consequences deprived the knights of their employment in imperial service, impoverished them and forced them to become robbers, in which capacity for centuries they committed the greatest atrocities against the German people. This had the consequence that the knights and the middle class became extremely hostile to one another, that a spirit of violence permeated all classes, and that the social tension between the upper and lower classes became more acute than in any other country. A main reason why no central Parliament could develop in Germany was the long degradation of the knights to a robber class, which unfitted them for political leadership. The German episcopate which was mainly in the hands of the nobility was deeply infected by its warlike and ruthless spirit and the lack of a strong central authority led to constant class struggles and to revolutions. In the towns the patricians overturned the rule of the bishops and nobles and subsequently their reign was overturned by the artisans. The peasants often rose against their lords and were defeated and cruelly punished. The fierce antagonism between the classes was later partly aggravated and partly replaced by the hatred between Catholics and Protestants. This mentality was the chief reason why Germany lagged so far behind other nations on the road to national unity and liberty. In France, national unity was at last restored and enlarged by the progress of royal absolutism, though at the expense of liberty. In Germany it was mainly the absolute power of the territorial princes which gradually succeeded in putting down anarchy, and in restoring a reign of law, though at the expense of unity and liberty.

The national differences in the position and mentality of classes and their in-fluence on the national character did not escape the attention of mediaeval writers. John of Salisbury (twelfth century) complains of the inefficiency and sluggishness of English military leaders in struggles with the savage Welsh, who were devastating English territory, and he praises the former warlike valour of the English which could be restored by training and discipline. He quotes Pope Eugenius III's opinion that the English were by nature better fitted than anyone for any enterprise they might choose if it were not for their levity. It was not military power, indeed, on which the English prided themselves, but their freedom, wealth and merriness. Henry of Huntingdon's famous praise of England as a free, merry, wealthy and generous country was repeated by numerous other English writers, and this view was also accepted by foreigners.

The interests of the lower classes were better protected in England by the Royal Courts than in countries where the central authority was weak. This was particularly noticeable in the French possessions and explains the popularity of English rule. An angry Count of Armagnac wrote to Henry III that under the rule of no other power did burgesses and rustics so domineer over nobles as in the territory subject to the king. Froissart[1] says that the English nobles were chivalrous and loyal while the artisans and common people were cruel, dangerous, proud and disloyal, and that the nobles were anxious to keep on good terms with them. They only demanded from the people what was reasonable and dared not to take an egg or hen without payment. In the fifteenth century Philippe de Comines, the adviser of Louis XI, admired the English Parlia-

---

[1] Jean Froissart, a fourteenth-century French chronicler and poet. — Ed.

ment, and pointed out that in no other country were public affairs better conducted and less violence committed on the people. Sir John Fortescue drew his proud picture of the constitutional monarchy in England which he contrasted with French despotism. While in France the people were terribly oppressed by the soldiery and by arbitrary acts of the government, the English people lived in security and were better fed and clothed than any other people.

The German and the French knights vied with each other in boasting of their pre-eminence in warlike virtues. Nevertheless, the Germans appeared to the other nations as particularly ruthless warriors. John of Salisbury comments bitterly on German arrogance and calls the Emperor Frederick I a "Teutonic tyrant." He also refers to King Louis VII of France, who was despised by the Germans resident in Paris because he lived like a citizen among his people, and did not appear in public guarded by an escort of soldiers like a tyrant going in fear of his life. Walter Map tells a story in which the English king is characterized by his wealth, the German Emperor by his military might, and the French by their enjoyment of life. An interesting tract, named *Noticia Saeculi* (1288), written by a German, probably Alexander of Roes or Jordanus of Osnabrück, discusses the diversity of national characters. The author finds that the Italians are ruled by the economic instinct, the Germans by the lust of domination, and the French by their thirst for knowledge. This leads to the predominance of the people in Italy, of the warriors in Germany, and of the clergy or the scholars in France. Each nation shows many good and bad traits corresponding to its fundamental tendency and the ethos of its ruling class. The author describes these traits in great

detail and some of his observations still agree with views widely held to-day.

Towards the end of the Middle Ages the German knights, according to Froissart, had a very evil reputation for ruthlessness towards their enemies and for neglecting the code of chivalry. Philippe de Comines describes the extraordinary number and violence of the robber-knights in Germany who have little to fear from the princes, as these need their military services in their wars. In 1519 Erasmus wrote to a friend that he had discovered such brutes among Christians as he could not have believed to exist. The disorder in Germany was partly due to the natural fierceness of the race, partly to the division into so many separate States, and partly to the tendency of the people to serve as mercenaries. This tendency maintained itself for several centuries longer.

The internal wars and insecurity that reigned in France and in Germany in the Middle Ages led to the foundation of numerous fortified points of refuge which later developed into towns, and also other reasons fostered the growth of towns. The feudal disintegration of the central government, furthermore, gave many towns the opportunity of winning an almost republican independence. This movement went farthest in Germany, where the reign of violence and the weakness of the Government were particularly pronounced, while in France the rise of royal power increasingly restored peace and restricted municipal autonomy. In England, where conditions were more peaceful, urban development was much slower than in Germany, except in London, and the English towns were always firmly under the control of the central government. Some of the German town-republics achieved a remarkable development of wealth and civilization which aroused the greatest admiration of such foreign observers as Aeneas Silvius, Machiavelli and Bodin. The German merchants for some time played a paramount role in English trade and finance, and Edward III even pawned the Crown of England to them for a loan. Many German towns, moreover, became great seats of industry and the Germans excelled in many crafts and manufactures. The fundamental differences in the social structure of the nations also expressed themselves in the sphere of industrial evolution. In Germany the great demand for armour, swords and other implements of war, together with natural conditions, stimulated the rise of the iron and metal industries, of mining, and of machinery for these productions. The Free City of Nuremberg became the foremost place in Europe for mechanical products. In England natural and social conditions fostered the rise of sheep farming and later of the cloth industry. In France the ascent of royalty to power was connected with the development of artillery for the royal army, and of such luxury industries for the Court and the aristocracy as silk, glass and porcelain. The national peculiarities in the field of industry which developed many centuries ago to some extent still characterize the economic life of the nations at the present day.

Although feudalism was a decentralized governmental system, it promoted the idea of national unity. Through a hierarchy of personal ties between lords and vassals, culminating in the king, feudalism brought allegiance to something beyond one's immediate lord and local loyalties and thus prepared the way for nationalism. The author of this interpretation, THOMAS F. TOUT (1855–1929), best known to historians for his studies in medieval administrative and political history, was professor of history at Manchester University.*

Thomas F. Tout

Feudal Allegiance
and National Sentiment

England and France were more alike in the Middle Ages than they are now because mediaeval conditions were similar in all Western Europe. A chief reason for this was that there were few of those differences between one land and another which are brought about by differences of nationality. There is a bad habit of reading present conditions into a remote past from which even historians are not free, though they have less excuse for it than other men. It has resulted from this habit that we are accustomed to apply our present conception of Europe to mediaeval times. We think of Europe as consisting then, as now, of independent units called nations, each of which has its separate history and traditions, each of which is, or imagines itself to be, of a common stock, each of which speaks, or claims to speak, a dominant national tongue, and each one of which is, or hopes to be, the basis of a self-sufficing national state. It is hard to say what constitutes a nation. For the present it is hardly going too far to say that each local group, which believes itself to be a nation, has a very reasonable chance of becoming one. We are seeing at this moment one regrettable result of this process. The doctrine of nationality, which for a hundred years has been the rallying cry of political unionism, is in grave danger of being the pretext for a dangerous disintegration of Europe into states, not strong enough to live a dignified and self-respecting

*From Thomas F. Tout, *France and England: Their Relations in the Middle Ages and Now* (Manchester, England: Manchester University Press, 1922), pp. 5–15. Footnotes omitted.

national existence, and still less able to constitute sound economic units. In their broad lines our recent treaties have been an attempt to extend the sphere of the national state, partly by readjusting the political boundaries of existing states to suit national conditions, and partly by extending to the many potential "nations," notably those till yesterday unequally yoked together under the Hapsburg crown, the principle of nationality which hitherto they have been unable to realize. But in no mediaeval treaty—nay, in no modern treaty before the nineteenth century—did any politician dream of making an attempt to shape the boundaries of states so that they should correspond more accurately with the nations. More than that, it was not until quite modern times that the ideal of the national state had presented itself, save to a few dreamers.

The Middle Ages were familiar enough with the word "nation" (*natio, nation*). If they seldom came across the name in their Virgil or their Ovid, they could read about the nations in their Cicero and their Caesar, and they occasionally found the word in their Latin Bibles, which they read much more often than they read the poets, orators, and historians. But in all these places the word "nation" was destitute of any political significance; it hardly ever had anything to do with the state. It was sometimes used to denominate vaguely a group of people which might be sometimes, but which more often were not, members of the same political community. Sometimes it was employed more specifically to denote a minute political entity that could in no wise be described by moderns as a nation. Thus the poet Dante writes of the "Slavs, the Hungarians, the Germans, the Saxons, the English, and other nations," as if the Slavs had ever been a political state, or as if the

subordinate Saxon nation did not convey quite a different sense of nation to that involved in its application to the nation of the Germans. Elsewhere Dante described himself as a "Florentine by nation," as if a city state and a national state could be regarded as identical. Clearly "nation" here means sometimes a race, sometimes a state, and sometimes a subdivision of the state. But "nation" was used in other senses as well. There are passages where the tenants of a monastery are said to belong to the "nation" of their house. There are others where the "nations" mean the common people, the *tiers état*. ["Third Estate"—Ed.].

The most general use of the term is to indicate a district, or the people of a district. It was in this sense that the well-known use of "nation" to describe the four "nations" of Germany was made. This was also the sense in which the word "nation" was employed to denote the subdivision of the students of a university. This use began in Italy, where the numerous foreign students who studied at Bologna grouped themselves into clubs called "nations," according to the districts, cisalpine or transalpine, from which they came. When the term was artificially applied to the students of Paris, it resulted in their arbitrary division between four such accidental "nations" as the French, the Normans, the Picards, and the English. There can be nothing political in a list which includes so divided a community as the Picards, or which strove to group the cosmopolitan crowd which flocked to the schools of Paris from the whole of the western world into four such "nations" as these. Whatever "nation" meant to the mediaeval mind, it at least never meant anything that in any wise corresponded to the modern national state.

If we would, then, appreciate rightly

the relations of England and France in the Middle Ages, we must begin by clearing away from our minds the modern doctrine of nationality as the normal basis of the political state. We must not assume a Europe split up into separate and self-sufficing unities called nations, and still less must we imagine that political relations, and even the social and economic relations that depend upon politics, could be determined in the long run by the ebb and flow of national sentiment. In modern times it may be recognized that some nations have natural affinities towards others, and therefore tend to have relations of friendship between each other. Others, on the other hand, regard certain states as natural enemies from generation to generation. More often, however, the policy of interests prevails over the policy of traditional likes and dislikes. As the national interests vary or remain constant, so do the dealings between the states embodying the national aspirations. Hence the extraordinary fluctuations that we know too well in the mutual relations of the states of Europe with each other. There was plenty of warfare in the Middle Ages, but it is only at the very end of that period that we can imagine these wars as the result of national sentiment.

Mediaeval man was clannish, local, limited in his attachments. He felt the reality of membership of the same community, but the community which made a real claim on his sympathies must be tangible, small, ever present before his eyes. Mere local proximity was not enough, for there might well be the deadliest conflicts between neighbours, since their interests were more likely to clash in proportion as they lived side by side and had different ends in view. Thus it resulted that the active and potent political relations of the Middle Ages were those which were based upon a small scale. A man felt loyalty to his native town or village and to the lordship, county, or other small organization of which he was consciously a part. He could be a Londoner, a Parisian, a Florentine: he could be a West-Saxon, a Norman, a Breton, or a Bavarian. But he found it hard to feel that he had any obligations as an Englishman, a Frenchman, or a German.

There was, however, one special loyalty to which mediaeval man could effectively respond. This, if in many cases serving as a new link in local and clannish attachments, might on occasion prove a real step towards the establishment of a larger allegiance and make, therefore, towards a broader unity. This was the personal tie of devotion to a common lord. That lord might be the village squire: but he might also be the ultimate ruler of a wide district—a king, a prince, even an emperor. And this bond of lordship was particularly strong in the case of the personal servants of such a lord, his *familiares,* the members of his household or *familia.* Accordingly, the most potent force that made for larger unions in the Middle Ages was the tie of lordship. This was the more felt since the lord was proprietor of the soil as well as political ruler, landlord as well as king. In this sense "feudalism" made for a real union. In its higher ranges subjection to a common lord made for national unity: in its lower ranges it made for the local unity which prepared the way for national unity. Indeed, the development of the great monarchies, from which the modern national state was ultimately to arise, would have been quite impossible had it not been that each mighty local lord had been doing within his own sphere what the kings themselves had to do within wider limits. It is not only the Capetians and the Valois who built up the French state. The dukes of

Brittany and Burgundy, the counts of Champagne and Toulouse, even the English dukes of Guienne, each prepared the way for the realizing of the ultimate ideal by establishing a well-ordered consolidated central power within his own appointed limits. Hence the importance of the smaller aggregations. Hence the constant use of the word "nation" in the sense of province—that is, some district subject to a common lord and having some local feeling of unity. With all his vagaries M. Flach[1] has done good service to scholarship in emphasizing the vital part of what he deftly calls *les nationalités régionales* ["regional nationalities"—Ed.] in building up *la nationalité française.* ["French nationality"—Ed.].

We may claim, then, that feudalism prepared the way for nationalism, alike by promoting the unity of those smaller aggregations which facilitated the growth of the national state and by bringing together the future nations under a common tie of obedience to an ultimate lord. Yet it must not be supposed that feudalism as a whole made for unity. On the contrary, the feudal baron presents himself in history as an eminently disruptive force. His ideal was that there should be as many kings as there were lords of castles. This conception was fatal to all good government, for the lord of a castle was, as a rule, proprietor of an estate too small to give him the resources necessary for becoming an effective ruler. As such he was the natural enemy of strong government, which could only be secured by a monarch, wielding extensive resources over a widespread territory. Feudal privilege, which arose from the dissolution of the imperial world-state of the past, was equally incompatible with the universal political unity of Roman tradition and

with the national state of the future. Moreover, feudalism was a force common to the whole western world. It made for cosmopolitanism rather than for nationalism, for it was in itself an instrument for levelling up all Europe by the wide diffusion of a common ideal. The feudal baron, the feudal castle, feudal justice, land tenure, and all the rest were part of that common European heritage which still remained a potent fact, even after the break-up of the Roman Empire had destroyed the political unity which in the early centuries of the Christian era made the whole western world subject to a single state.

This political unity was, moreover, but one side of the picture, and, as time went on, it became the less important side. The Catholic Church was even more cosmopolitan than feudalism, and it was the church, rather than feudalism or the empire, which had now become the chief effective force in keeping the western world together as a single community. Yet the church, like feudalism, was in some ways a disruptive force. It was the church, with its claim to immunities more comprehensive than the franchises of the baron, that had made all ordered political rule difficult, since in its zeal for marketing out in grand lines the things which it claimed to belong to God it unduly restricted the sphere which it allowed to Caesar. The church, no less than the baron, was the natural enemy of the king. "All the progress," as M. Génestal[2] has well said, "all the progress of the royal authority may be summed up in these two phrases—a victorious struggle against the law courts of the feudal lords, a victorious struggle against the jurisdiction of the church."

---

[1] Jacques Flach (1846–1919).—Ed.

[2] Robert Génestal (1877–1931), a French medievalist and student of legal history.—Ed.

Plenty of hard things have been said as to the dangers of feudalism; much, too, has been said as to the anti-social activities of the mediaeval church. But in recognizing their weaker sides, let us not be blind to the forces emanating from them which made for order and progress. Civilization is the resultant of many potent contributory elements, some of them contradictory to others, but all of them working for progress. Even feudalism, the "organization of anarchy," must not be too unsparingly condemned. The rabid anti-clerical interpretation of mediaeval history is always in danger of becoming a mere travesty of the facts.

Thus there were many factors contributing to the development of civilization. But of the men wielding these instruments we may feel sure that most of the makers—royal, ecclesiastical, provincial, or baronial—of the modern nations were labouring with absolute unconsciousness of what was to be the result of their efforts. They worked, moreover, not for society but for themselves. Regarding themselves as proprietors of their respective jurisdictions, they were urged, both by duty and interest, to make their dominions strong, united, and prosperous. Their motives, in short, were the same as those of the great vassals who had prepared the way for them. Yet when, as in the age of Phillip the Fair and Edward I, they had established a real domination over an ordered and centralized community, the kings of the nations commanded allegiance much more as supreme lords than as political sovereigns. Great kings did not differ in kind but in degree from their nobles. Both classes alike accepted that identity of the economic with the political wherein lay the very essence of feudalism. Every western land was subject to similar conditions of government. Everywhere was there an aristocratic class of great landed proprietors, who ruled over their landed possessions as princes. All these monarchs, great and small, governed both their domains and their whole dominions by the instrumentality of their household servants, and it was from the organized household of mediaeval potentates that the modern ministries, the modern fashions of administration, had their origin. They did not distinguish between the management of an estate and the government of a principality.

Under these conditions the principle of allegiance remained personal rather than local. The Middle Ages reprobated as an inquity treason against the lord: they had not yet begun to appreciate the enormity of treason against the community, the betrayal of the interests of the nation to the foreigner. Indeed, the "foreigner" was to the mediaeval man much less the alien of a distant land than the neighbour with whom he had to have constant dealings but with whom he could never agree. England, the first of the nations to raise an outcry against the foreigner, remained one of the most sympathetic lands to the alien who identified himself and his interests with his new domicile. Thus the England of Henry III exhausted its vocabulary of invective against the Poitevin and Savoyard kinsfolk of king and queen who strove to exploit the land in their own interests. Yet England willingly followed the leadership of a pure Frenchman, such as Simon de Montfort, when he put himself at the head of the national party of opposition. The rivalry of family with family, of district with district, of class with class within the same region was much fiercer than strife with distant lands about which the ordinary man knew little and cared less. It seems an astonishing thing to the modern Englishman that the barons, who had wrested Magna Charta from John, should have called in the future Louis VIII, the heir of the French monarchy, to save English·liberty from the English tyrant. It seems scandalous to the modern Frenchman that a great Norman baron, like Godefroi de Harcourt, should in 1346 invite the English into Normandy. Even more bewildering to modern patriotic emotion is that Anglo-Burgundian alliance of the fifteenth century which, for a time, threatened to remove France from the list of independent nations of Europe. But to the Middle Ages both seemed natural enough, and no worse a crime than the ordinary "defiance" by a vassal of his lord. In the same way there seemed nothing monstrous to the fourteenth-century mind that the king of England should claim the throne of France because of some imagined right of descent which, if established, might perhaps have given him a claim to a landed estate. But a kingdom was a landed estate to a mediaeval eye, and men saw no harm in anyone demanding his legal rights.

Even in the thirteenth, still more in the fourteenth, century it was becoming clear the proprietary monarchy was not enough. The instinct which rallied England to expel Louis of France in 1217, the foresight which in 1327 led the barons of France to repudiate the insidious doctrine that marriage might give a legal right to a foreigner to dominate their land, showed that national feeling was beginning to assert itself.

ERNST H. KANTOROWICZ (1895–1963) was
successively professor of history at the University of
Frankfort, the University of California, Berkeley, and
the Institute for Advanced Study at Princeton, New
Jersey. A specialist in the field of medieval political
theory and law, he here relates those subjects to the
larger issue of nationalism. He concludes that the
deliberate use of propaganda by French monarchs
intent upon rallying public opinion around the royal
banner was a significant step in the creation of national
feeling.*

Ernst H. Kantorowicz

Patriotic Propaganda

In 1302, after the bull *Uniam Sanctam*
had been hurled against the secular governments at large, and against France in
particular, after Philip IV had summoned the first Parliament of the three
estates of France to bolster his position
against the pope by a public manifestation from the whole kingdom, and after
the king, in his disastrous campaign
against the craftsmen and peasants of
Flanders, had suffered the terrific defeat
at Courtrai (July 11, 1302), an unknown
French cleric delivered a sermon on the
departure to war of a royal army. The
sermon may have been designed to intensify the political propaganda which
the king was then releasing. Philip ordered prayers throughout the country;
he made, in a somewhat modern fashion,
a general appeal to the *amor patriae*
["love of country"—Ed.] of all his subjects;
he raised new funds for the continuation
of the war, and asked subventions from
all, including the clergy, "for the defense of the native fatherland." That
the term *patria* then did not mean
the native hamlet, village, or province,
but meant the whole kingdom of France,
is not only implied, but this time also
stated *expressis verbis* by one of the outstanding legal councilors of the Crown,
William of Nogaret. He repeatedly declared that he, Nogaret, like everyone
else, was ready to defend, together with

*From Ernst H. Kantorowicz, *The King's Two Bodies: A Study in Mediaeval Political Theology*. Copyright © 1957 by Princeton University Press, pp. 249–258. Reprinted by permission of Princeton University
Press. Footnotes omitted.

65

the Catholic faith and unity of the Church, "his king and his fatherland, the realm of France," and that he himself as a knight was willing to die to defend *patriam meam regnum Franciae* ["my country, the kingdom of France"—Ed.], explaining on one occasion—like other jurists—that in defense of the fatherland it was a merit rather than a crime if a man killed his own father. Without going to these extremes, the French bishops, following the doctrines of the canonists, were nevertheless bound to admit in a letter to the Holy See that the ecclesiastical privileges and immunities had to be suspended when all the forces of France were mobilized *ad defensionem regni et patriae* ["for the defense of king and country"— Ed.]. Actually another great French jurist, William Durandus, Bishop of Mende,[1] had discussed in his *Speculum iuris* ["Mirror of the Law"—Ed.], some twenty years earlier, the extraordinary steps a king was entitled to take *pro defensione patriae et coronae* ["for defense of country and crown"—Ed.]—a not uncommon juxtaposition of "fatherland" and "Crown" which naturally made *patria* synonymous with the whole kingdom or body politic over which the "Crown" or its bearer ruled.

Within this general propaganda action —uniting the king, the legists and the reluctant bishops—the sermon of the unknown French cleric of 1302 has its place. He preached on I Maccabees 3: 19–22:

They march against us in the plenty of pride and lawlessness. . . . *We*, however, will fight for our souls and laws; and the Lord himself will crush them before our faces.

It was a suitable text for a patriotic proclamation and it had been selected by others before, a text which would lend

itself probably in any century as an ideal motto for justifying any war in a self-righteous fashion.

To prove the righteousness of the French and the just cause they were fighting for, the preacher started by exalting the saintly character of the *nobiles et sancti reges Francorum* ["noble and holy kings of France"—Ed.]. The French kings, said he, were saints (1) for the perfect purity of the blood royal which was holy because purity itself was a kind of holiness (*puritas quae est sanctitas quaedam*), (2) for their protection of holiness with regard to the Church, (3) for their spreading of holiness by siring new saints, that is, holy kings, and (4) for their working of miracles. These arguments were current and ever repeated in the year of nascent dynasticism in France when the king's *sancti praedecessores* ["holy predecessors"—Ed.] were invoked with the same ease with which in the Hohenstaufen circles the emperor's *divi praedecessores* ["divine predecessors"—Ed.] were remembered. That the French *reges christianissimi* ["most Christian kings"—Ed.] were the hereditary special protectors of the Church was an ancient claim which, for obvious reasons, had to be reiterated in a campaign pretending to protect the Church and the true faith against the pope. The royal miracle of healing scrofula, the "king's evil," was a popular topic of preachers and orators to prove the French king's general superiority over other kings and his spiritual sovereignty within his realm. Only the claim saying that the *sancti reges Francorum* also "begot holy kings" seems to carry slightly further than usual some essentially familiar ideas of that age; it may have been inspired by Vergil, who called the young Trojan Ascanius, Aeneas' son, a "son of gods and sire of gods to be"—a verse which had been effective in Antiquity and

---

[1] William Durandus lived *ca.* 1237–1296.—Ed.

which was now applied, not unsuitably, to the French dynasts who, according to popular sagas, could claim Trojan origin and trace their descent from King Priam.

From the holiness of the dynasty the preacher could easily make the deduction *a fortiori* ["with stronger reason"—Ed.] that the cause of "holy kings" could not be but the cause of Justice herself. Naturally, the Flemings were fighting for an unjust cause, since the French were fighting for the just one—*cum autem nos bellemus pro iustitia, illi pro iniustitia* ["moreover we fight for justice, they for injustice"—Ed.]. The wicked Flemings were almost to be congratulated, though, because through a war carried against them by a king who was a saint, they had a fair chance to be, as it were, "liberated" from their injustice. Better to be conquered by the holy king of France than by some wicked philosophy of life or by Evil itself—an idea, reflecting the doctrines of scholastic philosophy, which conveniently put the Flemings in the position of political and moral "infidels" and made the war a crusade for justice.

Moreover, the preacher asserted that the king's peace—the necessary corollary of the King's justice—was the peace not only of the kingdom of France but also of the Church and of Learning, Virtue, Justice, and that the peace of the realm would permit the concentration of forces for the sake of the Holy Land. To stress the cultural and educational mission of France had become a fad, at once aggressive and politically important, in an age in which France was generally, even by foreigners, given credit for having almost monopolized the *studium,* just as Italy harbored the *sacerdotium* and Germany the *imperium.*[2] Also, to make the plight of the Holy Land a lever for foreign and home policy was a strategem used incessantly by France in the second half of the thirteenth century, and by others as well. Finally, the oneness of French issues and Church issues, always strongly emphasized, was a most effective means of political propaganda in the days of Philip the Fair: *Pax regis, pax vestra; salus regis, salus vestra* ["The king's peace is your peace; the king's welfare is your welfare" —Ed.] was the key-note for nationalizing the clergy and gallicanizing the Church of France. Hence, it was not difficult for the preacher to draw his conclusion straightforwardly:

He that carries war against the king [of France], works against the whole Church, against the Catholic doctrine, against Holiness and Justice, and against the Holy Land.

Here a general equation of anything with everything has been achieved: war for the king, war for France, war for justice, war for culture and education, war for the Church, war for the Christian faith—all these were interrelated, interdependent arguments placed on the same general denominator. We can hardly be surprised when we find another preacher of those years proclaiming that "properly speaking, no kingdom should be called *regnum Franciae* except the Kingdom of Christ and the blessed," thus projecting the holy realm of this world into the other world as the model of the *regnum coelorum* ["heavenly kingdom"—Ed.]. Already we seem to hear the iron-clad maid of Domremy[3] saying: "Those who wage war against the holy realm of France, wage war against King Jesus."

Even that bulky freight of moral-political ideas interspersed with religious

---

[2] That is, the "educational function," the "priestly function," and the "political function" respectively — Ed.

[3] The French national heroine Joan of Arc (1412–1431). — Ed.

values was not beyond enlargement, for the preacher was capable of integrating yet another argument. As might be expected he demanded from his compatriots readiness to suffer death, if necessary, for the holy king of France. He demanded such willingness not on the grounds of the old feudal ties between lord and vassal, but on the grounds of "natural reason" and of the organological concept of the state. Natural reason, argued the preacher, dictates that all limbs of the body not only be directed by the head and serve it, but also be willing to expose themselves for the head. The head of the realm is the king. Therefore, any part of the realm that assails the king, assails the head and ventures to destroy the whole body and finally himself. To fight for the body politic of France meant, at the same time, to fight for the cause of justice as represented by the holy king. Consequently, to those killed on the battlefield for that just cause, spiritual rewards were promised such as would be granted to the crusader.

Since the most noble kind of death is the agony for justice, there is no doubt but that those who die for the justice of the king and of the kingdom [of France] shall be crowned by God as martyrs.

In other words, death on the battlefield for the political *corpus mysticum* ["mystical body"—Ed.] headed by a king who was a saint and therefore a champion of Justice, became officially "martyrdom." It equaled the self-sacrifice of the canonized martyrs for the *corpus mysticum* of the Church, the head of which was Christ. The "agony for justice," exemplified by Christ, was the price paid for the national martyr's crown and palm branch, even though "justice" meant, purely and simply, anything that was expedient, according to natural reason, for the body politic

of France and its head, the holy king. In the garb of justice the idea of "reason of state" began to betray itself.

In all this, as throughout his sermon, the preacher echoed only thoughts which others, too, had expressed, including the king and his councillors. *Quisque teneatur patriam suam defendere*, "Every one shall be held to defend his fatherland," declared William of Nogaret, a statement which certainly agreed with legal opinion and with the customs of France around 1300. Ever since the battle of Bouvines in 1214, the armed contingents of citizens formed part of the royal armies. In addition to the third estate, however, the clergy too ranged as "limbs" of the national body politic of France, and like ordinary citizens they had to contribute at least financially to the burden of defending the French *patria* and with it the Gallican *corpus mysticum*. Philip himself threatened to confiscate, in 1302, the possessions of those refusing to observe the king's orders of embargo and thus to contribute to the defense of the realm, because those "deserters of the fatherland's defense" were not worthy to enjoy proceeds and returns resulting from the efforts of all and from the burdens shouldered by others. The organic-corporational concept, looming in back of King Philip's decree, was actually asserted with greatest precision in a pamphlet of 1296, pretending to be an answer to a papal letter in connection with the taxation of the clergy. The pamphlet itself was apparently composed by one of the royal legists, probably Peter Flotte, who bluntly declared:

Depraved is the part that does not conform with its whole, and useless and quasi paralytic a limb that refuses to support its own body; layman or cleric, nobleman or man of low birth, whoever refuses to come to the support of his head and his body, that is, the lord king and the kingdom [of France], and lastly of himself, proves to be a non-conforming part and a useless and quasi paralytic limb.

The royal legist thus stigmatized "non-conformance with the body politic of France" as an offense almost of *laesa maiestas*[4] of which, according to this interpretation, the Roman Pontiff had tried to make the Gallican clergy guilty. To parry those efforts, the French jurist drastically called upon the organic nature of the French kingdom. The Gallican clergy, which together with the French laity formed the "Gallican Church," was exhibited as an integral part of the body of *patria*—limbs of the French body politic, no matter what in other respects the clerics' place may have been within the mystical body of the universal Church. By thus levelling the Gallican clerics to the status of French nationals the author succeeded in transcending, at least politically, the dualism of clergy and laity, not by the *corpus mysticum* of the Church, but by the mystical *corpus politicum* ["political body"—Ed.] of the French *patria*. The *corpus mysticum patriae* ["mystical body of the fatherland"—Ed.] was set over against the *corpus mysticum ecclesiae* ["mystical body of the Church"—Ed.].

---

[4] "lese majesty"; an offense against a ruler's dignity as head of the state.—Ed.

In this essay the British historian, GEORGE G.
COULTON (1858–1947), late professor of history at
Cambridge University, surveys the late medieval
church and relates the various crises through which
it passed—the Babylonian Captivity, the Great Schism,
the conciliar movement, and, finally, the Reformation
—to the development of nationalism. Note that Coulton
uses as evidence of medieval nationalism the writings
of people Kohn earlier dismissed as being atypical of
medieval men. How can historians reach such different
conclusions about what is typical or atypical of an age?*

George G. Coulton

The Papacy

Within less than half a generation from
Salimbene, Pierre Dubois was writing
his *De Recuperatione Terrae Sanctae*
["On the Recovery of the Holy Land"—
Ed.] [1305–7]. The Hohenstaufen Empire
was then dead, and most European countries had already coalesced into something like their modern forms; therefore
with these more definite nations we now
get a more definite nationalism. The old
struggle between Empire and Papacy is
now a new struggle between France and
the Papacy. Not, of course, that it is yet
the definite self-conscious France of modern times. The "public opinion" which
Dubois sought to mould was, in effect,
only the opinion of King, nobles, and
higher clergy, with a few rich merchants.

Yet, in seeking to mould, he is evidently
taking for granted certain pre-existent
tendencies and prejudices in this "public"
of his; and, when we look outside that
narrower field, would it not be rash to
assume that the lower clergy and the
mass of Frenchmen, in so far as they
thought of these matters at all, would
have differed far from their betters?

War, says Dubois, is universal; we live
in a world of perpetual and unabashed
vendettas. There are wars between "patri-
archs, primates, archbishops, when they
are enfeoffed with dukedoms, earldoms,
baronies, and other temporal things."
France and England, however, are hap-
pily exempt; there these quarrels are
fought out in the law-courts. The teach-

*From George G. Coulton, "Nationalism in the Middle Ages," *Cambridge Historical Journal,* (1935),
34–39. Reprinted by permission of the publisher and Professor Coulton's literary executor. Footnotes omitted.

ings of Holy Writ and of pacifist preachers "suffice not, and have not sufficed; and, even though they may have suffced at some places and times, yet in very few, as compared with the whole world of the Pope's subjects." Moreover, innumerable examples prove that this is due to "the want of provision and ordination in the head that is set above so many members."

If the holiness and teaching and prayers of the holy fathers [in past times] have not made wars and perils of wars to cease among Catholics, how can the Pope presume that the prayers and teaching of present-day and future ministers of the Church will put an end in future to the wars and greed and avarice wherefrom wars spring?

The Church, by the evil example she thus sets, is in a sense guilty of *lèse-majesté* against Christ her King. The fear of hell is less operative than temporal penalties; therefore what we need are tangible sanctions; for instance, boycott of the offenders, or interference by neutrals in the cause of peace. The Pope must be protected against his own warlike temptations by a system which, while leaving him enough of his revenues for spiritual work, would put the secular executive of the Patrimony of Peter into commission, under one or more national sovereigns: "thus the Pope, who ought to be the agent and promoter of all peace, will not wage wars and make men to die in battle by sudden and awful death."

If, then, the One Church is so inadequate for the task of European peace, Dubois naturally falls back upon nationalism. He is very conscious of the differences, and therefore of possible misunderstandings, between English, Germans, Spaniards and French. Moreover, the French have long been baulked of their full place in the sun. They have had very few Popes

by reason of the cunning and the natural guile of the Romans, who, striving in their pride to tread under foot the humility of the French, have presumed to attempt (a thing hitherto unheard of!) to claim temporal dominion over the realm of France and its sovereign prince, damnably inciting that realm of greatest peace and concord to perpetual sedition.

Therefore, "since the Roman Pope has abused his power, and has abused it as a Roman," it is only just that the Romans should be unwillingly compelled to admit a series of French Popes. Then "if the Lord Pope remain long in the realm of France, it is probable that he will create so many French cardinals that the papacy will remain among them and will escape from the so ravenous hands of the Romans."

The further Dubois pursues his argument, the more definitely does his nationalism come out. France is the natural and inevitable leader of Crusades: Dubois had not forgotten Guibert's *Gesta Dei per Francos*. Yet it will be better for her king not to risk his life there, as St Louis did; let him rather guide his armies from afar, so that he and his son may

live long within his own realm and dwell there rather than elsewhere, and also beget their children in the neighbourhood of Paris, so that they may be born and nourished there, seeing that this place is notoriously subjected to a better constitution of heaven than any other places whatsoever; whence it followeth (as hath hitherto been seen) that men begotten and born there are of better composition, order and complexion than folk of other regions.

They "far surpass all others in manners, constancy, bravery and beauty, as hath been proved by natural experience." Therefore

it would be expedient for the whole world to be subject to the realm of the French, provided always that the King be begotten, born, and brought up and instructed, according to wont, in that realm. . . . Certainly the French make far surer use of reasonable judgement than any other nations whatsoever, nor are they moved by disorderly impulses; seldom or never do they fight against true reason; a quality which we see not among other folk.

I have heard it pleaded that, in Dubois, this very emphasis of nationalism betrays it as factitious: that we have here a special pleader attempting to kindle the flame in a hitherto inert mass. Yet at least such a mass must be combustible; predisposition must be there; and it is very difficult to believe that, if Dubois had taken these theses for the text of a harangue in any market-place of France, he would have found one man in a hundred to contradict him. Indeed, Dr Previté-Orton[1] suggests to me the contrary probability: that barons and high ecclesiastics were far more internationally-thinking and internationally-disposed than the common man, in so far as the common man ever thought of anything outside his own village. And we know what a crop of deeds came from this seed sown not only by Dubois, but by other contemporaries whom we can name and many more (in all probability) who have left no trace in written records. Jean de Jandun,[2] some twenty years after Dubois, preached to the same effect: "The universal monarchy belongs to the most illustrious king of France, at least in virtue of a native leaning towards that which is best."

For, when Dubois wrote, the backswing of the Papal national pendulum had already begun.

---

[1] Charles W. Previté-Orton (1877–1947), an English historian best known for his constitutional studies and his concise abridgment of the *Cambridge Medieval History*.—Ed.

[2] Fourteenth-century French cleric, scholar, and teacher at the University of Paris. Jean was an associate of Marsilius of Padua and associated with the antipapal party of Louis of Bavaria.—Ed.

The idea of nationality had come, and was invading even the Faith. The Pope had become all but identifiable as a French prince, and the German spirit was in revolt against this. The captivity of Avignon had begun under Clement V in 1307; the protest of Louis followed in 1323. The episode occurred at the very moment when nationalism as a new ideal was effervescing to a head. The consequences were obvious and immediate. St Catherine saw that the one thing that could save the Church was to bring the Papacy back to Rome, to establish publicly its international character.

We have there only one side of the truth, even if it be the more important side. As Dubois shows, this French nationalism of 1302 was partly the fruit of a long process which had limited the Papal tiara to the single nation of Italy or even the narrower area of the Roman States. We may safely say *nation* in this connexion, since, as we have seen, although Italians were politically disunited, they could inspire a general repulsion in outsiders. So far, then, was the Papal return to Rome from healing these national rivalries, that it would seem rather to have increased them. The one colourable excuse for those cardinals who finally supported the French anti-pope was that they had heard the mob bellowing all night long under their windows: "A Roman, a Roman, we want a Roman for Pope, or at least an Italian!" Then,

When the schism was declared and the two parties stood in avowed opposition, allies began to gather round each from motives which were purely political. Italy took the side of the Italian Pope, except the kingdom of Naples, which had been closely connected with the Papacy at Avignon, and so maintained its old position. France laboured for Clement VII, to assert its former hold upon the Papacy. England, through hostility to France, became a staunch partisan of Urban, when Scotland declared itself on the side of Clement. If Urban, by his unyielding behaviour to Giovanna, had estranged Naples, he had by his complacency secured Germany. One of his first acts had been to accede to the request of the Emperor Charles IV that he would recognise his son Wenzel as King of the Romans: the death of Charles IV on November 29, 1378, set Wenzel on the throne of Germany. Hungary took the side opposed to Naples: the northern kingdoms went with Germany; Flanders followed England through its hostility to France; the Count of Savoy adhered to Clement, whose kinsman he was. The Spanish kingdoms alone remained neutral, though in the end they fell into the allegiance of Clement.

For, by this time, the nationalism towards which Europe had been evolving for three centuries past was accepted not only as a social fact but as a fundamental factor in European politics. The Great Schism was ended, not by blinking the facts, but by an attempt to transcend them. Here was "the first of European Congresses; a meeting of national delegates rather than a parliament of Christendom." Following the immemorial Parisian tradition, and voting by nations, the Council of Constance thus associated rival countries in a great common purpose; associated them systematically and juridically in a rudimentary League of Nations. But Popes, in the long run, were able to outplay those Constitutionalists; the League failed, and national rivalries became worse than ever.

Here, again, France and Italy supply the clearest example: and the facts are stressed by another eminent Roman Catholic historian, P. Imbart de la Tour. We are, by this time, on well-trodden ground; but it is worth while to follow this particular thread in a book so learned and so clear. Imbart emphasizes the omnipotence of French royalty from the later fifteenth century onwards: "this monarchical unity is a national unity in the making." Louis XII "appeals to national

feeling against the English, or to religious hatred against the Turk." The "nationalization of commerce" proceeds apace: "as early as 1517, it drove·the government to a system of absolute prohibition" of Franco-English trade. Dr Postan, again, emphasizes the part played by nationalism in Anglo-Hanseatic relations. He premises that "we know very little, much less than historians often assume, about the medieval conceptions of state and nationality; and until we know more all the discussions of economic nationalism are bound to be somewhat unsubstantial." Yet, with this warning, he goes on to speak of "the nationalistic bias of the times"; the English merchants' policies were "fashioned on definitely nationalistic lines," and those of the Hansa, apparently, no less so. This same process was going on everywhere in Europe; and (as Imbart observes) it reacted upon the Popes. Under Julius II (1503–13)

the Italianization of the Papacy was complete.... A French, German, English or Spanish pope would always have been suspected of serving the interests of his own country. An Italian Pope, by reason of the divisions and [political] unimportance of the Peninsula, could no longer cause offence. Rome "nationalized" herself in order to maintain the internationalism of religion amid the greed of the States.

Thenceforward (except for Adrian VI, 1522–3) all Popes are Italians. And thus deep calls unto deep; this nationalized Papacy provokes even more definite nationalism in the States. We find in France a quasi-separatist movement which may now be quite definitely called Gallicanism. "The separation, independence and sovereignty of the two powers, Priesthood and Royalty, form the doctrine—we may say the primary doctrine—of our Gallicanism." The Pope is "in the Church, but not above her": "his Primacy does not give the Pope power to modify arbitrarily the statutes of particular Churches." Thus, in no country was national feeling before Henry VIII so strong as in France.

But the same process was going on, more or less, everywhere. It was inevitable, in a world where, on the one hand, nations were gaining that inner cohesion which is a natural step forward in civilization, and, on the other, there existed no central power to which men could confidently look for the reality (as apart from the pretence) of international justice. Treaties have never been very secure in any age; but perhaps there has been no later time in which the historian may more confidently repeat Imbart's excuse for Louis XII:

In a century in which superstition allied itself with every crime and cloaked every perfidy, he was humane; and, if he broke his word, it was for the good of France, with her complicity, and with the excuse of an age when the art of negotiation was but the art of betrayal.

And, if we look beyond Imbart's special field, we find everywhere "those monarchies, powerful at home, jealous of foreign interference, which contributed so much to the Reformation." Those German princes who, when once the religious revolution was accomplished, agreed on the principle *Cujus regio, ejus religio,*[3] were lineal descendants of those who had witnessed the Lügenfeld, and who in later ages had suffered the cruellest civil wars through Papal decisions or indecisions which had been too obviously conditioned by Papal, and not by international, interests. Therefore, in so far as either can be said to have made the other, it would seem far less true to say that Luther created nationalism, than that centuries of growing nationalism produced a Luther.

---

[3] This principle, giving each ruler power to establish in his state the religion of his choice, was put forth in the Peace of Augsburg (1555).—Ed.

The universal claims of the Church and, in particular, the political power of the papacy often are thought of as forces inhibiting the development of nationalism. This thesis is challenged by FREDERICK HERTZ, who sees the Church as the institution that first encouraged people to think of themselves as Germans, Englishmen, Frenchmen, and so on, and then, having done this, resisted their "national aspirations."*

Frederick Hertz

The Role of the Medieval Church

The Roman Church has often been described as the implacable enemy of nationality. Professor Masterman,[1] for example, says:

The two great enemies of nationality in history have been Imperialism and the Roman Catholic Church. And in both cases the hostility has sprung from the same cause—distrust of the value of freedom. The Roman Church has been in the past a magnificent foster-mother of nations in their infancy, but she has resented and resisted their efforts to grow into manhood.

In spite of the admission about the past,

---

[1] John Howard Masterman (1867–1931), Anglican bishop and historian who studied church-state relations in medieval and modern times.—Ed.

however, this view needs considerable qualifications. In the Frankish Empire, and in other States too, the Church was at first quite dependent on the Government, while in Anglo-Saxon England State and Church were almost fused but under the practical guidance of the Church. In the course of development Church and State everywhere contended for predominance, and it was often doubtful which side defended the really national cause. The supra-national character of the Roman Church worked for the unity of Christendom and in particular of Christian Europe, but it also fostered the formation of wider and firmer regional communities out of the chaos of tribal and feudal diversities and rivalries. These

*From Frederick Hertz, *Nationality in History and Politics* (New York: Humanities Press, Inc., 1944), pp. 114–118. Reprinted by permission of Routledge and Kegan Paul Ltd., London, and Humanities Press, Inc., New York. Footnotes omitted.

traditional differences seemed of minor importance to ecclesiastics who regarded Christianity as one great mystical organism. St. Thomas Aquinas wrote: "Though one distinguishes peoples according to diverse dioceses and states, it is obvious that as there is one Church there must also be one Christian people." It was the Church that first looked upon the English, French and German peoples as units, which combated the existence of different tribal laws in the same territory, each valid for members of a specific tribe only, and which in many ways furthered that spiritual, social and political unification that led to the ideal of nationhood. To the Teutonic and feudal tendency of regarding Government as a profitable appurtenance of landed property, she opposed the idea that it was primarily a responsibility to God. The Teutonic custom, therefore, of dividing a realm on the death of the king among his sons was combated. The feudal tendancy of separating the classes to such an extent that the unity of the people was almost wiped out also met with the opposition of the Chruch. Many ecclesiastical writers such as John of Salisbury compared a people to a great organism in which each organ depended upon all the others, and which formed an indissoluble unit. After the Norman conquest of England the Church bridged the gulf between the ruling and the subdued people, and brought about their amalgamation. In Italy, however, the Papacy was an obstacle to political unity since this would have threatened its position. Moreover, the Church greatly enhanced the authority of the kings by the rite of coronation and consecration, giving them in this way a divine sanction, the position of a magistrate instituted by God. This too strengthened the forces making for unity. But the Church was far from thereby proclaiming the king an absolute ruler. According to ecclesiastical doctrine neither the king nor the people was sovereign in the sense of unlimited power, an idea also incompatible with that of an organism. Both were subject to divine and natural law, and the Church claimed to decide whether this law had been infringed, and, if necessary, to order redress. At the coronation of every king the officiating bishop asked whether the people consented. The people present, of course, were the great nobles who were thought to represent the rest. Yet the principle was implied that the people was the source of royal power and that the will of God acted through the people.

The rise of the Papacy to monarchical power, and the development of Church law, administration and finance served as a model for the rulers of states. Most of their great ministers and advisers were ecclesiastics and many of them were foreigners or of low birth. These men created the institutions which became fundamental to the development of modern states and nations. They not only laid the foundations of monarchical power but also had a great share in preparing and developing parliamentary institutions. The origin of the English parliament, in particular, was to a very large extent due to the counsels of Churchmen, and in Simon de Montfort's parliament the lords spiritual had an extraordinary predominance over the lay lords.

The evolution of England and France towards nationhood was greatly furthered by the fact that their relations to the Papacy remained comparatively undisturbed by the great struggles between the Emperor and the Pope for supremacy which had such a fatal influence on Germany's national unity. In these struggles the Popes frequently supported or even aroused national and democratic aspirations of the peoples against the emperors. They, furthermore, claimed suzerainty over a large number of states, and this was not merely an outcome of their striving for domination but was also meant as an encouragement of forces striving for freedom. The Popes stood not merely for the enhancement of their own power, they also stressed the pre-eminence of the spirit over the sword; and their combat against worldly rulers was largely directed against their claim to use the Church like a profitable property in the interests of their dynasty, and their helpers, the feudal nobility. Gregory VII, the son of a peasant, wrote to a German bishop: "Who does not know that kings and princes descend from those who, disdaining God, and persuaded by Satan, the lord of this world, were striving with arrogance, malignity, murder and every sort of crime to domineer over human beings, their equals, driven by blind passion and unbearable presumption." The revolutionary pathos of these words reveals the theocratic origin of later democratic ideas. For centuries the political life of the Italian cities and States was dominated by the struggle between the Imperial and the Papal party, the Ghibellines and the Guelphs, in which the former usually consisted of the aristocratic class and the latter of the more democratic elements. John of Salisbury taught that a tyrant who violated the natural law might be deposed or even killed, and Aquinas seemed to approve this principle. Manegold of Lauterbach[2]

declared that the people had the right to chase away a bad king as a farmer had the right to turn out a bad swineherd. Later on many ecclesiastical writers proclaimed the sovereignty of the people though subject to eternal law.

While the Popes were the first to appeal to the peoples in their struggles with emperors and kings, these soon took their revenge by appealing to the peoples against the Popes. There has almost always been rivalry between the temporal and the spiritual power, between the warrior and the priest, and this antagonism was rooted both in the divergency of ideals and in the clash of interests. These struggles frequently assumed the character of a combat between the national and the supra-national principle, especially when representatives of the nation, or the clergy of a country, took the side of the king against the Pope. Other issues, however, were often connected with the demand for nationalization of the Church like that of general Church reform, or the striving for influence over the Papacy. The movement for nationalization started in England, and soon made great progress in many countries. The grievances against the Papacy were financial, political and spiritual. The Popes tried to maintain the clergy as a separate body within the nascent nations, as a State within the State, dependent on their command and contributing exclusively to their treasury. Their international policy often conflicted with national aspirations. The corruption of the Church was notorious. Moreover, the greed of kings and nobles for appropriation of ecclesiastical wealth and power, and the commercial middle classes' jealousy of the Church caused by economic competition, were important factors. The Papacy suffered a crushing defeat at the hands of French royalty, and

---

[2] An eleventh-century canon regular who supported the papacy during the Investiture Controversy. Manegold was the author of a polemical treatise promoting the contractual theory of kingship. — Ed.

for a long time was degraded to an instrument of French policy. The movement culminated in the Great Schism and in the Councils of Constance and Basle. The Reform of the Church failed largely through the Anglo-French antagonism in the Hundred Years War. But the Popes made compromises with the rulers which gave them large powers over the Church in their states. Many factors combined to foster the rise of national states, ambitions and rivalries, and to prepare for the advent of the Reformation.

GAINES POST (b. 1902), professor emeritus of history
at Princeton University, has distinguished himself
in the field of medieval law. In this study of the
writings of a Spanish lawyer he shows how the "reality"
of medieval nationalism was paralleled by the
"theoretical" arguments of the legist. On the basis
of these he concludes that the concept of universalism
as represented by the Holy Roman Empire was
seriously challenged in law by the claim of Vincentius
Hispanus that Spain was an independent kingdom.
Moreover, Post says, the statements made by Vincentius
in support of his theory of Spain's independence reflect
"some nationalism in the modern sense of the word."*

Gaines Post

Legal Theory

In the Middle Ages the tradition of the
unity and universalism of the Roman
Empire was powerful, and it continued
in the mediaeval Roman Empire and the
Church as two aspects of the unity of
Christendom. But to which of all the peoples of Christian Europe should the empire and the office of emperor belong?
Pope Innocent III, in the decretal *Venerabilem* (1202), fully restated the theory
of Gregory VII, that in crowning Charlemagne as emperor, Pope Leo III had
transferred the Roman Empire from the
Greeks to the Germans. He and contemporary canonists generally assumed that
the German king who was confirmed by
the pope was, at least in temporal affairs,
the true emperor and lord of the Latin
West. Johannes Teutonicus, for example,
the eminent German canon lawyer who
in the first quarter of the thirteenth century taught at Bologna and wrote his own
and compiled others' glosses on the *Decretum* of Gratian[1] and the *Decretals* of
Innocent III, after stating the *translatio
imperii* ["transfer of the empire"—Ed.],
asserts that the German emperor is above
all kings and nations, for he is the prince
and lord of the world. The legists at
Bologna, steeped in the classical law of

---

[1] The *Decretum* was a twelfth-century compilation
of canon law with commentary which became the
standard legal text in schools and an authoritative
reference for ecclesiastical courts.—Ed.

---

*From Gaines Post, "'Blessed Lady Spain'—Vincentius Hispanus and Spanish National Imperialism in
the Thirteenth Century," *Speculum*, XXIX (1954), 198–209. Reprinted by permission of the Mediaeval Academy of America. Footnotes omitted.

the Empire, were naturally opposed to the idea that kings and kingdoms were independent of the emperor.

Nonetheless, the development of the feudal monarchies of England, France, and Spain, which were in fact outside the territories over which the German emperors nominally ruled, and the rise of a feeling of loyalty for native lands (occasionally expressed in the vernacular literatures as early as the twelfth century), foreshadowed the breakdown of the ideal of universalism. This was bound to happen even in the Empire proper, because of the bitter conflict between the Hohenstaufens and the papacy, during which particularism triumphed in Germany and Italy.

Quite early certain canon lawyers began to state the fact of localism in legal theory. Perhaps, as Sergio Mochi Onory has recently argued, they were eager to belittle the empire in order to exalt the spiritual universalism of the Church. More likely, however, the influence of local loyalty was at work. In the late twelfth and early thirteenth century several canonists argued that some kings have no superior, and are emperors in their own realms. Alanus, an English canonist at Bologna, clearly asserts that every king who is subject to no one has the same rights in his kingdom as the emperor has in the empire. The division of the world into kingdoms, he continues, was according to the *jus gentium*[2] and is approved by the pope, although by the ancient *jus gentium* there ought to be one emperor in the world. During the

thirteenth century the idea of the independence especially of England, France, the Two Sicilies, and Spain was increasingly expressed, particularly by Roman lawyers who entered the service of the kings. In England, Bracton, trained in both laws and a royal justice, likewise held that the king of England recognized no superior on earth. Francesco Calasso refuses to believe that *rex imperator in regno suo* ["the king is emperor in his own realm" — Ed.] meant independence of the Empire, for in a sense every local administrator was king or emperor in his sphere of jurisdiction, just as the *pater familias* ["head of the household" — Ed.] was king in his family and yet subject to a superior. But I find this argument weak: some canonists and legists, and theologians, held that the king, who had the powers of the emperor in his own realm, recognized *no* superior. We find, then, that the lawyers were thus beginning to state as legal fact the theory of independent kingdoms. Here was a legal basis for the claim of each kingdom to be an independent nation. Some nationalism in the modern sense of the word was reflected in the theory, and perhaps was intensified by it.

It is noteworthy that at the same time the lawyers began to associate such expressions as *res publica* and *patria* with the kingdom *(regnum)* and the idea of its independence. At first signifying on the one hand Rome or the Roman Empire, and on the other any lesser city or community within the empire, *patria* or *res publica* came to mean something else when associated with the independent monarchy. In the ideal of fighting for the realm as the common *patria* (instead of Rome), and dying for it (*Pugna pro patria* and *Pro patria mori*) one senses a feeling akin to modern, national patriotic zeal. It is amusing that a French canonist,

---

[2] *Ius gentium* is the law that is common to all men. It is derived from the common customs and usages among different peoples and is thus nearer to "natural law" than to any particular code of civil law. Today *ius gentium* is often used as a synonym for "international law," that is, the law that is common to all nations and peoples of the world. — Ed.

Guillaume de Montlauzun (d. 1343), accused Johannes Teutonicus of too much German patriotism *(favor patriae)* in championing the superiority of the emperor over kings. But he seems to reflect his own loyalty in supporting the idea that the king of France was emperor in his own kingdom, as French canonists and legists had been doing in the second half of the thirteenth century. Azo, indeed, although hostile to the theory, reveals that in the first years of the thirteenth century it had been argued that the king of France had the same powers in his kingdom as the emperor in the empire.

Now we must observe that in such statements there is no desire to give a king of France or Spain the title of emperor. The lawyers in favor of the national monarchies wish, instead, to show both that the king is independent of the emperor, and that his public authority is supreme in his own realm. But in the Iberian Peninsula the kings of Leon and Castile had since the tenth century sometimes assumed the title. In Spain, therefore, the idea already existed of an empire completely separate from the Holy Roman Empire of Charlemagne, Otto the Great, and Frederick Barbarossa. It had grown up partly in memory of Visigothic unity, partly (perhaps) in reaction against the claims of the successors of Charlemagne, and partly in the glory derived from the Reconquest. The culmination came in 1135, when Alfonso VII of Leon and Castile assumed the imperial title, and Pope Innocent II, perhaps intentionally, as a blow at the prestige of the Holy Roman Empire, allowed him to call himself King of Kings. St Ferdinand (1217–1252; 1230–1252 in Leon), fully worthy of the title, aspired to it, but apparently did not actually claim it. His son, Alfonso the Learned, was a candidate for the imperial title, not of Spain, but of the Holy Roman Em-

pire. But his efforts ended in fiasco, and during his reign he foolishly alienated those very attributes of the crown that pertained to the strength of the Castilian monarchy in Spain. "He aspired to be emperor, though he was not even able to play the king."

But if Alfonso X failed in this direction, in the *Especulo* and the *Siete Partidas*,[3] a great monument to his scholarly interests, he stated that the king recognizes no superior in temporal matters, and that kings have the same powers in their kingdoms as emperors have in the Empire—a clear reflection of the theory already current, as we have seen, among the canonists and legists. Thus the old ideal of an Empire of Spain surrendered to the newer theory of the national independence at least of Leon and Castile. Yet the older tradition of empire was nationalistic too. Indeed, Alfonso X departed from it in trying to win the crown of the Holy Roman Empire, and in a sense was ready to abandon the separate Empire of Spain for the mediaeval ideal of unity in the Roman Empire. The statement in the *Siete Partidas*, therefore, may be considered as a return, expressed in the formula *rex est imperator in regno suo,* to the tradition of Spanish imperialism.

Paradoxically, the ideal of the Spanish Empire was nationalistic. Yet there was no united kindom of Spain, and no king after the Visigothic period ruled over the whole Iberian Peninsula until the time of Philip II. If there was an ideal unity in memory of Visigothic Spain and in the goal of Christian reconquest, it never existed in fact in the Middle Ages. For despite the titles of emperor and king of kings, not even the ambitious Alfonso VII could rule over all the kingdoms that

---

[3] "The Mirror" [of the Law] and [The Law in] "Seven Parts."—Ed.

arose during the Reconquest. As a result, as the thirteenth century opened there were several kingdoms, of which the most important were Portugal, Leon and Castile, and Aragon. Nevertheless, the sentiment of unity connected with the idea of the Empire as a whole certainly persisted. We may therefore speak of a Spanish nationalism in the twelfth and thirteenth centuries.

If some of this nationalism is to be found in the Spanish chronicles, better evidence of it is furnished by a famous canon lawyer, Vincentius Hispanus. Where he was born is unknown, but probably somewhere in Spain. He studied and taught Canon and Roman law at Bologna in the late twelfth and early thirteenth century. He wrote glosses on the *Decretum* (1210–1212), a full *Apparatus* of glosses (1210–1215) to *Compilatio I* and also to *Compilatio III* (1210–1215); moreover, he glossed the Decrees of the Fourth Lateran Council of 1215 (1215–1216), and remained active as a scholar long enough to write an *Apparatus* on the Decretals of Gregory IX (hence Vincentius was active as a decretalist after 1234). His work shows special knowledge of places in Portugal (Braga, Coimbra, and Lisbon), where he held ecclesiastical provisions. In 1226 he was chancellor to King Sancho II, and was elected bishop of Idanha-Guarda in 1229. He died in 1248.

Despite his career in Portugal, there is no doubt that he looked upon himself as a Spaniard and was loyal to the idea of the whole Iberian Peninsula as Spain, of which Portugal was merely a part. He calls himself, in proper humility, "episcoporum Hispanie minimus" ["the least of the Spanish bishops"—Ed.] in the introduction to his *Apparatus* to the Decretals of Gregory IX. His glorification of Spanish virtues appears as early as 1210–1215: "With deeds, like a Spaniard," he says, "not with words, like a Frenchman." His praise of Spain begins at the same time, for he speaks of "noble Spain." He cannot accept Pope Innocent III's praise of the kingdom of the French. He declares that Spain, not France (the French Church), is greater than other ecclesiastical provinces, for "when Charles with all the northerners *(Francigenae)* wished to invade Spain, the Spanish blocked their passage, overcame them in battle, and killed twelve peers!"

These remarks were made, we have noted, about 1210–1215, and the last one quoted above is a gloss to the decretal, *Novit,* of Innocent III (1204). Yet, in this same period of activity as a decretalist, Vincentius had nothing of significance to say on Innocent III's still more famous decretal of 1202, the *Venerabilem,* in which the pope stated his version of the *translatio imperii* from the Greeks to the Germans. As we have seen, it was on the *Venerabilem* that Johannes Teutonicus, after 1217, offered his comment, that all kings and kingdoms are subject to the German, Holy Roman Empire. Why did Vincentius say nothing about Spain in reaction to a decretal that glorified the Germans, when he was writing his *Apparatus* to the *Decretals* of Innocent III and was sharply challenging the idea of the greatness of France? One cannot be sure, but the answer probably lies in Vincentius's resentment towards Johannes Teutonicus as a German patriot. Now, Johannes compiled the *Glossa ordinaria* to the *Decretum* shortly after 1215, and his *Apparatus* to *Compilatio III* (*Decretals* of Innocent III) after 1217, and in these works the German canonist made his sweeping arguments for the supremacy of the German Roman Empire. But Vincentius wrote the glosses in his *Apparatus* to *Compilatio III before* 1215. It seems likely, then, that his failure to react at this time against the right of the Germans to possess the empire and dominate all kingdoms comes simply from the fact that Innocent III in 1202 acknowledged that certain kings were independent of the emperor (in the decretal, *Per venerabilem*), and in the *Venerabilem* (also 1202) on the *translatio imperii* said nothing about kingdoms other than the German, while Johannes Teutonicus' opinions, moreover, were not written until after Vincentius commented on these decretals. Not even Laurentius Hispanus' work on the *Decretum* of Gratian and the *Decretals* of Innocent III (both before 1215), and his acceptance of the *translatio imperii* theory, aroused Vincentius—perhaps, again, because Laurentius did not specifically say, in his theory of the *translatio imperii* to the Germans, that all kingdoms are in the Empire.

But about 1217 Johannes Teutonicus commented on the *Venerabilem* in such a way as to call forth Vincentius' Spanish loyalty. Let us first examine the words of the German canonist, some of which have not hitherto been published. He declares that the government of the world was transferred to the Germans, although the Greek ruler could, *largo nomine* ["by extending the term"—Ed.], be called emperor, just as the king of chessmen can be called king, and that the true, German emperor is above all kings and nations; he is the lord of the world, all provinces are under him and all things are in his power (all this in the published portion of the gloss). Then he adds, "unless anyone shows that he is exempt." But no king can order an exemption, for in this he has as a subject of the emperor no power of prescription (limitation). Nor can any kingdom be exempt from the empire, because the empire would then be headless and, without a head, a monster. Indeed all *de capite suo* will pay

tribute to the emperor, unless exempt in this, as in *Dig.* 50, 15, 8 (on imperial grants of immunity to certain provinces and cities in Spain). All things are in the power of the emperor. "Let us acknowledge, therefore, that the Teutons by their virtues have won the empire" ("Fateamur ergo quod Teutonici virtutibus promeruerunt imperium").

Johannes Teutonicus thus glorifies the Germans by attributing to them the same virtues as those by which the Romans had originally built the empire—so Gratian, XXVIII. Q.I, c.14 Omnes, §Ex his: "iuxta illud Hieronymi, 'Virtutibus Romani promeruerunt imperium.'"

Perhaps an additional challenge was presented by Jacobus de Albenga, who commented on the *Decretals* of Honorius III (1226). Honorius III in the *Gravi nobis* (1220) warned the king of Portugal against imposing exactions on the clergy, and referred to the law of the emperor that granted immunity to the Church. To this Jacobus asks why the pope refers to an imperial law when the king of Portugal is not under the emperor; and he replies that although the king is not under him, he ought to be, and indeed "omnes reges debent subesse imperatori" ["all kings should be subject to the emperor" —Ed.].

But the flaunting of German superiority was more than enough to arouse Vincentius—he was easily moved! In fact it brought forth an interpolation in the gloss of Johannes Teutonicus perhaps before 1234; in one manuscript I have found the words "excepto regimine hyspanie" inserted thus, "Sic enim regimen mundi, excepto regimine hyspanie, translatum est ad teutonicos ["Thus the government of the world, except the government of Spain, was transferred to the Germans" —Ed.]. If this insertion was not made by Vincentius (and there is no way of proving that it is his), he definitely revealed his indignation after the *Decretals* of Gregory IX were published by Raymond of Pēnafort in 1234. His comment is to the *Venerabilem* (*Decretals* of Gregory IX, 1, 6, 34) and it occurs in his *Apparatus* or commentary. So far as I know, his gloss has not been published.

Vincentius begins his remarks on the *Venerabilem* by quoting literally the earlier opinion of Johannes Teutonicus, namely, that the empire would be a headless monster if any kingdom were independent of it, that all men owe tribute to the emperor, that all things are in his power, and that by their superior virtues the Germans earned the empire. Now he gives his own opinion: "Make exception, Johannes Teutonicus, of the Spanish, who are exempt by the law itself [i.e., *Dig.* 50, 15, 8, on certain provinces and cities of Spain that were granted immunity from tribute to the emperor]! The Spanish, indeed, refused entrance to Charles and his peers. But I, Vincentius, say that the Germans have lost the empire by their own stupidity [does he refer to the excommunication of Frederick II by Gregory IX in 1239, or to his deposition by Innocent IV at the Council of Lyons in 1245?]. For every hut usurps lordship *(dominium)* for itself, and every city contends with others for the same. But the Spanish alone have by their valor *(virtute)* obtained the *imperium*, and they too [the Visigothic kings] have chosen bishops. In France, in England, in Germany, and in Constantinople the Spanish (are renowned because they) rule over the Blessed Lady Spain, of which they are acquiring the lordship and which as lords and masters they are expanding by virtue of their valor and probity. The Spanish, therefore, are aided by their merits and worth. Unlike the Germans, they have no need of a body of prescripts and customs.

Who indeed, Spain, can reckon thy glories? — Spain, wealthy in horses, celebrated for food, and shining with gold; steadfast and wise, the envy of all; skilled in the laws *(iura sciens)* and standing high on sublime pillars!"

To understand Vincentius' reaction and the context of his gloss, we must recall the Visigothic tradition and Isidore of Seville's encomium of Spain under the Visigoths, but above all remember that the period of his career as an important canonist, ecclesiastic, chancellor to the king of Portugal (1226 ff.), and bishop of Idanha-Guarda (1229–1248), was also that of great Spanish achievement. If the Albigensian Crusade resulted in greater power for the French monarchy and a check for Aragon in southern France, the victory of Pedro of Aragon at Las Navas de Tolosa (1212), and the expansion of Aragon under James the Conqueror into Valencia (1233–1245) and the Balearics (1229–1235) were adequate compensation. The Reconquest, moreover, was continued with brilliant success by King Ferdinand of Leon and Castile, who took Cordova (1236) and Seville (1248), and conquered Andalusia and Murcia, leaving only the small kingdom of Granada to the Moors. Despite the division of Spain into kingdoms, these were essentially Spanish victories and a legitimate source of Spanish pride. Spaniards, indeed, could boast that their participation in the Crusade of Christendom was as effective and glorious as that of the French and other northern nations in the expeditions to the Holy Land and Constantinople. Vincentius, I am sure, expresses the Spanish pride, nay, patriotism, that arose both from these and earlier achievements, and from the old tradition of the unity of Spain in the Spanish Empire. But the Germans of the same period were involved in futile wars in Italy, and Frederick II's Crusade of 1228–29 could hardly appeal to the Spanish ideal of fighting the infidel. Therefore the Spanish, not the Germans, possessed, like the Romans, those virtues by which an empire is won; and it is the Spanish, not the Germans, who have won and are adding to their empire. Such is the conclusion of Vincentius Hispanus.

But is this Spanish Empire a universal one that should take the place of the Holy Roman Empire and embrace all kingdoms and nations? Does Vincentius advocate imperialism, in the modern sense of the word, for Spain?

Alexander of Roes, in the later thirteenth century, ardently championed the traditional empire, but always in German hands: he wants no German nation or state like France; Germany must be above France (and other kingdoms); world imperialism belongs to the Germans. Thus he continues the ideal of Johannes Teutonicus. In France, a little later, Pierre Dubois countered with his famous plan for French domination in Christendom in order to assure the success of a final crusade. In both instances nationalism becomes a new universalism. But Vincentius had not gone so far. He glorifies Spain and the Spanish and believes that the Spanish are superior to the French and the Germans, and by their virtues merit the empire they have won and are expanding. This empire, however, is not the old, theoretically universal, Holy Roman Empire, which he would transfer from the Germans to the Spanish. It is, I feel, the Empire of Spain, of the Iberian Peninsula. His ideal, therefore, seems to be a continuation of the traditional feeling in Spain of the unity of Spanish history and civilization from the Visigothic period to the Reconquest. His ideal is no doubt limited, moreover, by the theory that the kingdom of Spain is

independent of the Holy Roman Empire, for the king recognizes no superior and is emperor in his own realm, and by his own belief that Spain was never ruled by Charlemagne. Not long after Vincentius died Alfonso the Learned was a candidate for the imperial crown, and perhaps he was inspired by some vague feeling that Spain should be the new center and controlling power of the Holy Roman Empire. Ultimately Spain was in fact the real center when in 1519 Charles I was elected emperor and became Charles V. Yet the true greatness of Spain had been and was being realized in the Aragonese empire in the Mediterranean, in the Portuguese expansion in Africa and the Far East, and in the Castilian conquest of much of the new world. The true Spanish Empire was only by accident joined to the Holy Roman Empire in the person of Charles V. It is with this Empire of Spain, not with Alfonso the Learned's abortive aspiration and the Empire of Charles V, that we must connect the fervid nationalism of Vincentius Hispanus. For the expansion of the Empire of Spain, independent of the Roman Empire, was in his time already nationalistic, and Spanish (Aragonese) supremacy in the western Mediterranean was beginning.

Vincentius Hispanus, then, offers one of the most interesting examples of the expression of the new feeling of patriotism and nationalism in the thirteenth century. His thought is the more remarkable because, as a canon lawyer, he should logically have believed in universalism not only in the Church but also in the State. Proud of Spain, however, and of Spanish achievements, he reacted against German boasts of supremacy. He reacted likewise against French pride. To any French claim of empire and domination in Spain, he responded by declaring that the French were full of words, not deeds, and that the Spanish had defeated the great Charles and killed twelve of his peers. Was Vincentius impatient with the *Song of Roland* and the French imperialism of the feudal epic? Was he simply reflecting Spanish dislike of those French knights who had often assisted in the Reconquest and whose conceit and arrogance frequently aroused resentment in the twelfth and thirteenth centuries? Or was he acquainted with the legend of Bernardo del Carpio in the chronicle of Rodrigo of Toledo (1180–1247; Rodrigo studied at Bologna and Paris, and was bishop in 1209) or with an earlier version of the story told in the *Poema de Fernan Gonzalez* (1250–1271) of how Bernardo defeated Charles and the twelve peers? Whatever the causes of his national pride, Vincentius will have none of France nor of Germany and the Holy Roman Empire. His common fatherland, his independent kingdom and empire, is Spain — Noble Spain, Blessed Lady Spain!

The obligation of freemen to defend the realm provided a common experience for a portion of England's population and indirectly produced a sense of national consciousness. Although weaker than the allegiance of modern man to the state, this new sentiment was the beginning of the end for the local and feudal loyalties of the early Middle Ages and thus a step toward nationalism. BARNABY C. KEENEY (b. 1914), formerly professor of medieval history and president of Brown University, is presently chairman of the National Endowment for the Humanities.*

Barnaby C. Keeney

England

The Victorians said much and assumed more about the English nation in the Middle Ages. They felt that it existed under the Anglo-Saxons, deplored its suppression under the alien heel of the Normans, rejoiced that Norman and Englishman were welded together in opposition to John, commended the wisdom of Edward I who gave the nation Parliament as its organ of expression, and finally acclaimed the emergence of the English nation in substantially its modern form out of the fiery crucible of the Hundred Years' War.

The modern reaction against the assumptions of nineteenth-century scholarship has undermined the belief in the existence of any sort of nationalism in the Middle Ages. Recent authorities hold that three forces prevented the development of true national feeling in the early Middle Ages. The claim of the universal Church on man's higher loyalties prevented them from being attached to his own country. The universal language, Latin, prevented the stimulus to national feeling that comes from a patriotic national literature. Poor communications and limited circulation prevented the common man from becoming aware of his nation, much less attached to it. His limited horizon combined with feudal and manorial loyalties to produce provincialism rather than nationalism.

* From Barnaby C. Keeney, "Military Service and the Development of Nationalism in England, 1272–1327," *Speculum*, XXII (1947), 534–549. Reprinted by permission of the Mediaeval Academy of America. Footnotes omitted.

These assumptions of universalism on the one hand, and localism on the other appear contradictory. They are, moreover, only partially true. The Church was indeed universal, but even churchmen thought of themselves as Frenchmen or Englishmen. As the Middle Ages wore on, men came to be dominated less by religion and more by secular considerations. By the end of the thirteenth century, the number of secular-minded men was considerable. Latin was the universal language of scholars, but they were a small minority of the population. It is apparent that some men who wrote in Latin thought in the vernacular. Vernacular tongues were used by all men in their daily intercourse. By about 1300, serious as well as popular works were written in England in the vernacular tongues, both French and English. Localism persisted in England until modern times, but from the twelfth century on, the expansion of the royal court and with it the royal authority tended to break down provincial loyalties and made men aware of the king and his central government.

The reaction has gone too far. Nationalism in its extreme modern form did not exist in the Middle Ages with demands on loyalty excluding all other loyalties. There was, however, a feeling of obligation to the king and to the community of the realm that came between the two extremes of universal loyalties on the one hand, and provincial and feudal attachments on the other, and which was one of the causes of the break-down of these two attachments and the rise of modern nationalism.

Many of the symptoms of nationalism are evident in England at the turn of the fourteenth century. The consciousness of kind shared by a large group of people united in one state is present in the concept of the community of the realm. A nation feels that it is entitled to determine its own destiny, and sometimes the destiny of inferior peoples. From the reign of Henry III on, the barons, at least, felt that they were entitled to work out the country's destiny with the king, and without any outside help. There is a suggestion that the English thought they had a mission to rule the other peoples of the island. Co-nationals ordinarily speak the same language: it is clear that nearly everyone born in England at the end of the thirteenth century learned to speak English, though he might prefer French or Latin. Documents and serious books were beginning to appear in English. English was the common language, but it was not to be the exclusive language for many generations, nor had the king's English yet suppressed dialects. The mythology of nationalism includes a belief in a common origin, real or fictitious. Edwardian Englishmen liked to think that they had a common origin with their fellow countrymen, even though they knew perfectly well that they were descended from different stocks. The historian Pierre Langtoft, who wrote in French verse for the upper classes, took great pains to show that Briton, Anglo-Saxon and Norman had fused to form the Englishman. In at least one instance, he deliberately falsified his source. His work was soon to reach a wider audience through the English translation of Robert Manning of Brunne. The most obvious symptom of nationalism in Edwardian England is dislike of foreigners, but it is the least significant, since it exists among nearly all peoples, even primitive tribes who have no feeling of nationalism. Dislike of real foreigners, as distinguished from the foreigner from the next village, was stimulated by the prominence of aliens in the entourage of Henry III and by the long series of foreign wars beginning in the reign of Edward I. National characteristics were already typed. Robert Manning knew "That frenche men synne yn lecherye, and englys men yn enuye." Even patriotism was expressed by writers who were obviously influenced by the classics. Baker[1] described the Scots before Bannockburn as "Burning with love of their country's freedon, albeit unjustly." Yet the Scottish leaders may have been more opportunists than patriots, and many of Edward's troops in the Welsh campaigns were Welsh "friendlies."

These feelings existed, but they are of no importance historically unless they were concentrated in political channels, and unless the government used them to further its ends. Even today, emotions so vague and intangible as national feeling need symbols to give them concrete expression. In 1300, the symbol was the king. Loyalty to him was concentrated in the concept of the community of the realm, which was at its height. The king personified the country and, with the community of the realm (which was broadening out from the narrow baronial interpretation), was responsible as the protector and defender of his people, in whose interests he acted. Edward I put it thus: "The king has received the government of the realm by provision of God, by Whom he is held to the defense of the realm itself and of all his subjects, clerk and lay." More elaborately, Edward II said "We desire as befits royal majesty, and are bound by oath to maintain and preserve whole and unharmed the rights of our royal crown, our royal dignity, and the peace and tranquility of Holy Church and of the whole people committed to our rule, and to resist with God's help all

things which might occur to the weakening of the aforsaid rights or of our royal dignity, or in breach or disturbance of the peace, or terror of our people." On the one hand, the king regarded all the inhabitants of his realm as obliged to assist him in its protection; on the other hand, it was generally agreed that he was bound to exercise his powers for the common benefit of the realm and its inhabitants. His conduct, and even his household, were matters of general concern. Service was thought of as due to the king, rather than to the country, and offense was primarily against him, but since the king, his crown and his realm were really inseparable, treason came to be considered an act against the people as well as against the king. When Thomas Turbeville turned traitor for the king of France, Langtoft said that he worked to "make such despite to the English that King Edward would lose his land." Rebels were the "king's rebels" but they troubled the realm and its people as well as the king, and the people were expected to help put them down. To arouse feeling against Lancaster, and to get aid against him, Edward II published alleged copies of captured documents proving traffic between Lancaster's party and the Scots, showing that "they conspired to our shame and to the disinheritment of our aforsaid realm and the destruction of its people" by allying "against their liegances and fidelity" with the Scots our enemies. In another case, the treasonable agreement between Andrew Harcla and Bruce was in a very real sense a personal betrayal of the king who had made Harcla, but it was also regarded as an act against the realm and its people, even by the not unsympathetic author of the Chronicle of Lanercost.

The king used the feeling of obligation expressed through the community, and in so doing, increased its scope and in-

---

[1] Geoffrey le Baker, a fourteenth-century English chronicler—Ed.

tensity. Indeed, one of the roots of the feeling of community was the old royal encroachment in local government. By developing the common law and by extending the jurisdiction of the king's court until it included all freemen, the royal administration turned the loyalty of local people away from their feudal and manorial groups, and attached them to the community of the county, which was capable of representation in central assemblies. The participation of local men as jurors at the central court, and as representatives in Parliament not only broadened the viewpoint and loyalties of a very important and influential class but enlarged the *populus* that participated in government and, as the community of the realm, shared responsibility with the king for the preservation of the kingdom. The second royal policy that affected the development of nationalism was the practice of obtaining military service for the defense of the realm from large groups of men who had ro feudal obligation to fight. This in effect broadened the feeling of responsibility for the realm and its defense. Common service in warfare made men aware that they were part of something larger than their local community, and stimulated emotional attachment to the king and the country. The propaganda used to encourage service appealed to men's loyalty to the community, and at the same time, strengthened it.

The right and duty of all free men to possess and use arms to help the king defend the kingdom antedated and survived the conquest, and had been reaffirmed and used just often enough to keep the idea alive. Until the reign of Edward I, however, English kings had relied primarily on the feudal host supplemented by foreign mercenaries. The unpopularity of foreigners, particularly mercenaries, made it inadvisable to use alien troops in the Welsh and Scottish campaigns, which were very close to home, and military problems of organization, discipline and terrain made it impossible to rely wholly on feudal cavalry in these areas. Though both Edward I and his son depended heavily on a reorganized feudal array, Edward I revolutionized the English army by the introduction of large numbers of paid native troops under professional commanders. He was at once faced with two serious problems — finding natives suitably equipped and trained to serve as infantry or cavalry and persuading or forcing them to serve.

The natural source of heavy cavalry was the knightly feudal class. At first the earls and the greatest barons were adverse to serving for pay. The custom of securing the service of units of professional soliders by indentures was not fully developed until the reign of Edward III. In the period under consideration, commanders, knights and men-at-arms were recruited from the lesser baronage and the gentry. Neither their numbers nor their willingness to serve sufficed for protracted and frequent campaigns. Therefore, distraint of knighthood (forcing men to be knighted) was used to enlarge their numbers by requiring freemen of means, regardless of their tenure, to assume the obligations of knighthood, and to equip themselves as cavalrymen. Though distraint may have been used by the Angevins primarily to raise money through fines and compositions for failure to comply, as is sometimes stated, the Edwards used it chiefly to increase the supply of available men-at-arms and war horses. Assumption of knighthood was encouraged by offers of free arms supplied from the royal wardrobe. These new knights increased the numbers of available cavalrymen.

One of the most important trends in the development of mediaeval tactics is the increased use of foot troops. As early as the twelfth century, dismounted but still armored knights were used effectively. By the turn of the thirteenth century, men-at-arms, mounted and afoot, and infantry were used together under the leadership of knights. At the end of the thirteenth century, the development of the long bow provided the English infantryman with the efficient armor-piercing missile weapon that was to make him the superior of the armored knight, horsed or on foot. The longbow and the difficult terrain of Wales and Scotland combined to make the plebeian foot soldier, whose means did not permit the purchase of adequate armor, an efficient fighting man rather than the relative nuisance he had been hitherto. Any freeman was available for service, and was required by the Assize of Arms to possess weapons and armor in keeping with his income. This obligation was restated by the Statute of Winchester, but primarily to provide a force capable of preserving internal order against malefactors. In 1315, Edward II, who was fully aware of the original intent of that statute, consciously reinterpreted it to require the possession of arms "not only to preserve the peace of our realm but also to repel the Scots our enemies and rebels" since "in such difficulties and necessity . . . no one . . . can nor should be excused from those things that pertain to the conservation of our crown and royal dignity and the repulse of our said enemies and rebels." This and other similar proclamations used the statute as a basis for military service.

Both distraint and the reinterpretation and enforcement of the Statute of Winchester probably had the effect of increasing the numbers of men equipped for service mounted and on foot. The problem of getting them to serve was handled in several ways. Commissions of array were frequently issued giving commissioners power to muster the men of a county and to select a specified number of foot or horse to serve at the king's wages in a particular campaign, often outside of England. In an area threatened with attack, a custodian, captain or lieutenant was often appointed, sometimes at the request of the local people. He was empowered to raise all the forces of the county or other area involved. Service within the threatened area was ordinarily at the expense of the individual or local community, but the troops might be asked to serve outside at the king's wages.

Though both commissioners and captains were empowered to coerce, they seem to have negotiated with the local communities for grants of service. In 1299, Thomas de Furnivall was assigned to Nottingham and Derby to "select, try, order and assess men-at-arms . . . both foot and horse from all those who are aged between twenty and sixty" according to a scale of equipment based on income. Evidently, he negotiated a grant of service, because when the king later wrote him to alert the troops for service in Scotland, he said that "the men of the counties of Nottingham and Derby assessed for arms promised and conceded to us that they would be prepared to go with our person to the aforsaid parts of Scotland." In 1303 the county of Northumberland granted almost universal service in a meeting with royal representatives, and the county palatine of Durham granted men-at-arms and foot. In 1311, the counties were asked to grant the service of one foot soldier from each vill. They did so, but the service was cancelled, perhaps because of the opposition of Lancaster and other magnates. Such a grant was made in Parliament in 1316, but cancelled on grant of a sixteenth. A similar grant of service in 1322 was used. From time to time, the towns were requested to supply the service of a specified number of troops.

Year after year, the king raised sizeable bodies of troops, using not only his feudal right to service based on homage and fidelity, but his royal rights based on allegiance. He could not do this arbitrarily, since his rights to such service were not based on well defined feudal obligations. He had to negotiate and overcome opposition. It is characteristic of the period that most of the numerous requests for service, even feudal summonses, explained at length why service was necessary and why the individual should serve. The reasoning in the royal propaganda distributed to convince Englishmen that they should serve in war must have been founded on a knowledge of what was likely to arouse the emotions of the various classes of the population. There is no basis for the assumption that it is mere rhetoric. An analysis of this propaganda should cast some light on nationalism in this period.

Throughout these documents there is a recurrent appeal to the popular conviction that the king personifies the realm and is responsible for its defense, and that all his people are obliged to help him in time of need. He tries to identify the interests of the people with the interests of the realm. Sometimes the ideas are clearly expressed; more often they are merely alluded to or taken for granted. When Edward I wrote "What touches all shall be approved by all" and "common dangers should be met by measures provided in common," he was doubtless as concerned with common action as with general approval. In 1297, he ordered that all men with twenty pounds income (no

matter of whom they held their lands), prepare to serve wherever the king should lead them to defend the realm against the king of France, since "the matter is so great and thus touches all and each of our said realm, so that we can defer to no one." In the same year, he and his council ordained that the clergy pay a heavy subsidy since "his enterprises could not be successfully accomplished to the honor and profit and salvation of the king and his realm without the common aid of the clerks and laymen of his realm." Edward II appealed to the same principle of common obligation in requesting service against the Scots in feudal summons, in appointing captains for defense, in justifying his reinterpretation of the Statute of Winchester, and in asking help from the Church. He summed it up when he wrote, "Not only kings and princes presiding over their realms and lands, but also their subjects (*subditi*) in accord with the responsibility inherent in their position and the obligation of their fidelity are obliged to expend aid and counsel in accordance with their strength, whenever the occasion demands, to recover rights and kingdoms and other lands that have been taken away and wrongfully occupied." This doctrine of common obligation for defense was not new, nor was it peculiar to England. What was novel was a determined effort to enforce it on a national as well as on a feudal basis.

One of the most striking contrasts between the baronial and the royal theories of government is in their respective concepts of the realm. To the king, his realm embraced all his possessions; to the barons, it was a fief in which they held their own fiefs. The king's possessions outside England were other fiefs in which they were not obliged to serve unless they held lands there. Even before the loss of

Normandy, barons whose interests were mainly in England tried to avoid continental service. Once Normany was gone, few barons had any personal interest in the king's possessions on the continent, and it became more and more difficult to get them to serve abroad. The question of overseas service was one of the main issues disputed between John and the barons. It was not settled in Magna Carta, unless John's promise not to proceed against anyone without judgment was regarded as protection against arbitrary action for refusal to go to Poitou. John may have been trying to raise a substitute force in 1213 when he summoned all freemen for overseas service. It is generally believed that his chief desire was to raise funds, and he did take their expense money from the troops and send them home. It is possible, however, that he had intended to assemble and use a nonfeudal army, but dismissed the ordinary freemen when he saw they were an ill-equipped and disorderly mob, which they certainly were. The confused appeal of Henry III to the bishops for help in defending his "land of Gascony" reflects that king's desire to avoid raising the issue of the obligation to serve abroad on a feudal basis. Instead, he hinted at the common obligation to defend the realm. In 1297, when Edward I based his summons to the barons for foreign service on the general summons of that year, rather than on homage and fidelity, it was not his intention to commit an impudence, but rather to obtain the service "for the salvation and common utility of the realm," which he felt included Gascony, rather than have it denied him on the grounds that the barons, as vassals, were not obliged to serve outside England. This approach confused the barons, and they had difficulty finding other excuses. Had Edward succeeded in 1297, he and

his successors would have had available a force whose size would have been limited only by practical considerations, and whose service would have been based on allegiance—almost a national army. However, the acceptance of the obligation to serve at the king's command and at his wages was not far enough developed in 1297 to permit its application overseas. Edward and his son continued to regard Gascony and Scotland as part of the realm, and gradually they gained acceptance of the principle that Englishmen were obliged to serve outside England at the king's expense. The relation of this obligation to the duty to defend the realm of England is shown by the practice of paying troops after they crossed the border. In some of the Scotch campaigns of Edward II, troops served at the expense of the local community until they crossed the Tweed; after that, at the king's wages. In the futile Gascon campaigns of Edward II, barons and others served, but it appears that most, if not all, service was at wages.

In the first Parliament of Edward III, the protests against service abroad were renewed. Service overseas during the Hundred Years' War was on the basis of contract through indenture, not of national obligation. Thus, by 1327, the realm was tacitly defined as England, and all men were obliged to defend it. Troops raised to defend England against the Scots could expect to receive the king's wages if offensive operations into Scotland were undertaken. The obligation of common defense had never been seriously questioned; what had been debated was the extent of the realm. Thus, the king had to compromise to the extent that national service for the defense of the realm was restricted to England. He could raise troops to serve outside, but he had to pay them.

Since the king personified the realm, an offense against him was an offense to the realm. At first the Welsh and the Scottish wars were treated as a matter of rebellion by a vassal against his lord the king and throughout the struggles no opportunity was lost to describe Llewelyn or Bruce as a rebellious and treacherous vassal. This presentation should warn us against overestimating contemporary orientation towards nationalism. As the wars went on, however, the king attempted to arouse indignation by describing the ravages of the Scots. The account of their misdeeds was almost reduced to a formula, but new horrors were added from time to time. Though these very tangible offenses were most impressive to the inhabitants of the border, the royal propagandists must have believed that they would arouse the ire of any Englishman, for the documents describing them were used throughout the country.

In the Middle Ages, a people was most easily aroused by appeals to religion, as in the crusades against the Moslems, and in Germany against the pagan Slavs. All the enemies of England were Christians and not even heretics (though Philip the Fair was no friend of the Pope and Robert Bruce was excommunicated three times). Yet Edward II described the Scots as if they were pagans, whose purpose was to destroy the English Church both materially and spiritually. He declared that the Scots burned churches, shed Christian blood, and intended to "impose tribute on our people and Holy Church." The king of France was sometimes cast in the same role. It is curious to find two peoples of undoubted Christianity presented in this light; it shows the potent hold of religion on the popular imagination.

The task of the propagandist was easiest when there was threat, real or fancied, of an invasion. Both Edwards warned that the French intended to invade, with the purpose of extirpating the English tongue and of destroying the Church and the realm. Here the king had an ancient and undoubted right to call on everyone for defense, and since invasion was a matter of general concern and caused general fear, reference to it aroused popular emotion more readily than would allusion to an abstract belief, however widely held.

Thus, propaganda to raise troops was based in general on these three things: the honor of the king and the realm, the threat to Holy Church, and the obligation to help the king defend it and the realm against aggression. There was likely to be a difference of emphasis, however, in the appeals to different classes of the population. Summons to barons to render military service were no longer the terse orders of the Norman period, but were almost always prefaced by a more or less elaborate argument showing the necessity for such service. The prefaces were apt to be most flowery when they introduced a request for service beyond the *servitium debitum*—service at wages, or for service affectionately requested, to which the king was not clearly entitled. Since the audience thought in feudal terms, emphasis was likely to be given to feudal offenses, but not solely. The ravages of the Welsh and Scots, the threat of the king of France to subdue the realm, the danger to Holy Church, offenses and rebellions against the king were frequently cited, as was the general obligation to defend the realm.

In their efforts to establish the principle that churchmen were as much obliged to help defend the realm as laymen, the kings encountered much opposition. The position of the clergy was complicated by the policy of Boniface, on the one hand,

and, on the other, by the growing anti-papal feeling manifested in contemporary legislation and other documents. At the same time, prelates were of all people most capable of understanding an appeal to the duty of all to protect the state. The famous writ of 1295, with the *quod omnibus tangit* ["that which touches all"—Ed.] clause was addressed to the clergy. They were reminded from time to time that all were obliged to defend the state (*res publica*), and that since clerks could not fight, they ought to pay as well as pray. Likewise, they were told of the offenses against the Church, and reminded that the dangers and damages of an invasion would fall on them as much as on laymen. A royal order to the archbishop to convoke the clergy, transmitted down through ecclesiastical channels, was likely to receive very lofty additions as it passed from hand to hand, but it sometimes happened that the most elevated sentiments produced the least results or the most fervent denial of obligation.

Commissioners of array induced men to serve by verbal persuasion and by pressure rather than by documents and proclamations. The commissioners and those helping them were ordered to use every inducement to enlist men to fill their quotas and in one case they were instructed to offer bonuses. The men of the counties were sometimes flattered by receiving a royal commendation for their previous services shortly before the arrival of a commission. The commissioners must have used the prefaces of their letters of appointment as an outline of the points to touch on in their drive for recruits. These letters, and those to the sheriffs, which were published in the county, touch on all the points used in general to arouse people for service. The general obligation to defend the realm is implied but not emphasized. In 1322 the king ordered the alleged treasonable correspondence between Lancaster's supporters and the Scots published in the counties, probably to help commissioners arouse feeling against the rebels and the Scots and to facilitate recruiting. The eloquence of the commissioners was directed at the members of the county court, who probably helped make the actual choice of recruits, while coercion probably was applied to the men drafted.

In the letters appointing custodians, captains and lieutenants in areas threatened by invasion, reference was sometimes made to the common obligation to defend, and the emphasis was almost always on the actions and intentions of the enemy who was to be repelled. Though the captains and custodians had broad coercive power, it is evident that their efficiency depended largely on verbal persuasion, the details of which we cannot know.

When forces were raised from the towns separately from the counties, the local officials ordinarily did the recruiting, not royal commissioners. Royal letters were sent the mayor and aldermen, requesting them to fill a quota. In 1318 the letters reviewed the acts of the Scots, pointed out that the earls and barons had promised to serve in person, and went on to say "that for so great a necessity it is fitting to require and request that our lieges and subjects likewise lend helping hands." These letters were ordinarily the only means of persuasion.

It is difficult to determine how effective all this recruiting propaganda was. Service, military or financial, was not popular. The reaction of the baronage to what they considered an unwarranted demand in 1297 is well known. The clergy was equally unwilling to contribute in this year and in others. Among other classes, volunteers were not sufficient to fill the quotas, and wages and bonuses had to be supplemented by coercion. There were numerous desertions among the men from the counties and boroughs, and even among the barons. On at least one occasion a large part of a levy refused to serve. At times, lords of franchises obstructed efforts to recruit within their liberties.

This unwillingness to serve in the field would indicate a somewhat less than burning patriotism. Despite the small size of the forces actually in the field in this period, campaigns were so frequent that the draft may have fallen on much the same individuals more than once. It seldom takes more than one campaign to convince a sensible man that there are better ways of making a living than by military service. Such a conviction was reinforced by the confusion that characterized the wars of Edward II, who made and called off levies and even campaigns time and again. Those responsible for raising troops were not blameless; they accepted bribes and abused their power by drafting more than their quotas and then exacting fines for exemptions. The fact remains, however, that enough troops were raised to permit fairly continuous campaigning between 1282 and 1327.

These sources suggest that a step toward modern nationalism was made at the turn of the fourteenth century, but that the concept in its modern form did not really exist. Certainly there was nothing of the fanatical intensity of twentieth century nationalism. Nor can we argue that all Englishmen were affected, since the requests for service and the propaganda were addressed only to freemen— in practice, the more substantial freemen. Probably the mediaeval roots out of which our irrational devotion to the nation grew differ in kind, as well as in degree, from the modern conception. Rather

than devotion to the nation and the national state, we find loyalty and a sense of duty toward the community of the realm which was capable of developing into nationalism. The community of the realm consisted of individuals grouped into subordinate communities, such as the Church, the county, the borough and the baronage or peerage. The subordinate communities were in the process of breaking down, and the loyalties attached to them were being bound to the community of the realm and the king, its head and personification. Though the king still dealt with the subordinate communities as groups, he was beginning on the one hand to handle their members as individual subjects with common obligations, and on the other hand, to deal with the community of the whole realm in Parliament.

It is clear that feudal sentiments of loyalty were still important, but the tendency was to center them in the person of the king rather than in the immediate lord. Again, the appeal to protect the Church was used with effect. It is generally felt that a primary loyalty to religion indicates a lack of national feeling. Yet the Church to be protected is termed the English Church, and the people who were attacking it, though Christians, were foreigners—Scots or French. A feeling of what may, with great caution, be called national Christianity seems to be evident among both clergy and laity, perhaps partly as a result of the papal policy of treating large blocks of Christianity as provinces that corresponded roughly to political units. When the concept of the universal Church broke down, this notion of a national church might be a very important source of national feeling, and provide the emotionalism that was not yet associated with the lay state.

The importance of the community of the realm in the development of the national monarchy and of national feeling is indicated by the broadening of the meaning of the term itself. Earlier in the thirteenth century, it had referred to the baronage alone. By the end of the reign of Edward II, the phrase community of the realm sometimes identified the union of all individuals and subordinate communities, of which the baronage was one; in other texts it excluded the baronage and the Church, and meant the commons in Parliament, who represented most of the rest of the free population. There is evidence that peasants were loyal to the community long before they became an active part of it. The feeling of obligation to the realm by all the members of its community became an important factor in royal politics when the king found it worth while to appeal to it to gain support for his plans and policies.

The idea of the community of the realm and obligation to it gains significance in the history of nationalism because many of the secondary evidences of national feeling are associated with it. The English of the fourteenth century liked to think of themselves as one people with a fanciful common origin and a vague sort of destiny. They were thoroughly aware that they were Englishmen as well as Yorkshiremen; they disliked foreign foreigners more than they disliked the man from the next county. We find an anticipation of some modern nonsense when we read that "one Englishman can annihilate many Scots."

The characteristics of medieval nationalism, different from the modern variety largely in degree, are evident in France before the fifteenth century, argues the British scholar DOROTHY KIRKLAND. The components of modern nationalism were not, however, all present in the same place or at the same time in the Middle Ages, and it was the fusion of these elements that produced the unique state of mind we associate with nationalistic thought. In Miss Kirkland's opinion it is misleading to discuss medieval "nationalism" unless we distinguish between it and what is meant by the modern usage of the term.*

Dorothy Kirkland

France

[Albert] Guérard, in the first chapter of his book *French Civilisation from Its Origins to the Close of the Middle Ages* makes the arresting observation that apparently no civilisation reaches its perfection until, in point of historical fact, it has already been superseded. "Feudalism," he said, "did not find its complete expression until it had outlived its usefulness—such as that may have been. The theory of absolute monarchy was firmly established at last under Louis XIV: but it had already become a hindrance. Nationalism grew obscurely for many generations: it did not become dominant in men's consciousness until the nineteenth century, when the internationalism of science and industry was making it obsolete."

This is not so paradoxical as it seems, for the truth about life, as it is seen by men, is, broadly speaking, embodied in their social organisation; but to clothe ideals with their appropriate action is a slow process, and while it is going on, fresh truth may come to light. Since truth is essentially that which "makes sense" of all the data to hand, the accumulation of fresh data often calls for a fresh conception of truth. Small adjustments of this kind are made continually, without any serious challenge being offered thereby to the direction in which a civilisation is developing. But sometimes the new data are widely divergent from anything which the past had produced; the new exception may not only fail to prove the rule, but may actually prove it to be glaringly

*From Dorothy Kirkland, "The Growth of National Sentiment in France before the Fifteenth Century," *History*, XXIII (1938–39), 12–24. Reprinted by permission of the Historical Association. Footnotes omitted.

wrong. Then men are compelled to reconsider the whole fabric of life, and to acquiesce in large-scale alterations; but for a time the old social order will go forward, carried by its own momentum.

If it is true that no civilisation grows to completion before it has outlived its usefulness, it is at least equally as true that men do not begin to question a social organisation until they have outgrown it. They only become aware of a crop of problems inherent in the structure of their lives, when already that phase of civilisation is declining. When an age is troubled by irreconcilable paradoxes its end is at hand: the customary scheme of things has been thrown out of joint by the pressure of new ideals, and a fresh orientation of life is demanded. It is the beginning of the end: it does not happen while an age is in full vigour.

However full of contradictions the Middle Ages may seem to us to-day, at its best, medieval civilisation did not exhibit troublesome paradoxes to contemporary thinkers. That the paradoxes were there is beyond question. But it is when the Middle Ages are measured up against a standard that was unknown to them, and are regarded through alien modern eyes, that they seem to be full of motley confusion. There is ample evidence that, until certain fresh elements came to disturb them, men were content with the world as they found it, organised on a feudal basis, with the Church as the great unifying factor. They were not aware of the contradictions which disconcert us. There came a time, however, when these problems loomed large, because new disintegrating elements were forcing themselves upon the notice of thinking men, and of these new forces none was so powerful as that which we have come to know as patriotism.

Even a cursory survey of the writings left to us indicates quite clearly that something was definitely changing men's outlook. Compare, for example, two sets of verses written at, roughly, the distance of a lifetime from each other. The *Combat de Trente* (1350–51) gives a very fair picture of a feudal combat, thirty knights a side. True, one side is French and the other English, and the English leader says that Edward will win all the land and become King of France, only to be met with the retort that he should dream again, for that is a bad dream. But there is no rancour, or bitterness: the important thing is that all knights, no matter which side they are on, shall behave with true valour. The poem ends with praise for them all, and a prayer for the souls of all the slain of both companies.

Compare this with some verses discovered at Valence. . . . This "Ballade contre les Anglais" ["Ballad against the English"—Ed.] (dated between 1428 and 1430) belongs to another world of thought. Its opening lines set the key:

> "Ariere, Englois, couez ariere!
> Vostre sort si ne resgne plus."[1]

The verses which follow play upon themes familiar, in later days, in patriotic songs—the special favour of Heaven to the one side, and the pride and wickedness of the other; rejoicings that the enemy is being deserted by all except scoundrels, and gleeful satisfaction at the ills which have befallen his army. The struggle is no longer a courtly joust between knights bound by a mutual code of honour: it has in it the venom of a life-and-death struggle between two peoples. The English are not only enemies; they are foreigners, men of another "sort." National sentiment is becoming articulate.

What, then, is national sentiment? Dictionary definitions vary widely, but there is fairly general agreement that

---

[1] "Away English, take yourselves away/You have no future here."—Ed.

patriotism includes: (a) love of the soil, of a certain prescribed area of land with its scenic characteristics; (b) appreciation of an agreed way of doing things in general, including language and art; (c) loyalty to a centre of government embodied, in the first instance, in the person of a ruler who is frequently a hereditary king, though later this devotion may be extended to a governing body; (d) finally, a willingness to sacrifice personal comfort or advancement for the sake of these loyalties.

Not until at least these four elements have become fused, and the resulting state of mind is widespread amongst a people, is it anything but misleading to use phrases about love of country, patriotism and national sentiment, unless quotation marks are inserted to indicate that something different from the modern content of the words is implied.

It is beyond question that the search for such a synthesis in medieval times is vain, but the different elements are to be found, singly or in combination, centuries before the final fusion takes place. Take two examples.

The *Chanson de Roland*, in spite of its origin in folk-song, cannot with any vestige of truth be dubbed a patriotic poem. Yet it is the *Chanson de Roland* which coins the phrase "la douce France" ["sweet France"—Ed.]. The dying Roland is not longing for a political state, or a nation, but for the gay green earth of France.

Or again, when in his "Virelai contre le pays de Flandres,"[2] Eustache Deschamps praises "ce doulz pais de France" ["this sweet country of France"—Ed.]; or when he writes a ballad with the refrain:

"Riens ne se puet comparer a Paris" ["Nothing can be compared to Paris"—Ed.]; he is not merely praising the land, but the French way of life. Yet the idea of sacrificing his own interests for the good of France as a whole simply never occurs to him: even the royal command to remain in his own proper district and perfrom fully his duties as bailiff makes him furiously angry. The implication of service following appreciation appears to be foreign to the mind of Eustache Deschamps.

Even when national sentiment, in its full meaning, has come into existence, it is liable to fluctuate. At one time an absorbing interest, at another it becomes submerged. Weak and often negligible in times of prosperity, it will flame up fiercely under the stress of adversity. "The force of nationalism in the Middle Ages," W. T. Waugh writes, "has often been underestimated by modern writers who, accustomed to its extravagant manifestations, have supposed that, where it was not the dominating influence on men's actions, it did not exist at all. . . . It may be strong in one country and absent in the next. It may determine the conduct of a people at one time, and then be superseded by another force. In the Middle Ages, it was seldom very powerful, but it is a mistake to suppose that it was wholly absent. It is doubtless true that it often grew out of unworthy passions, if indeed it is not an unworthy passion itself."

To some this last suggestion may seem a hard saying, yet even the most enthusiastic patriot would be compelled to admit that whenever any national sentiment comes into existence, its first and most obvious result is contempt for, and disgust at, "the foreigner." He is hated not because he has done evil, but because he is different, and whenever this spirit

---

[2] "Refrain against the country of Flanders." Deschamps was a late-fourteenth-century French poet—Ed.

is exhibited it is safe to infer a certain rudimentary nationalism.

In Princkmeir's *Troubadours,* under the name of Jubinal, there are verses entitled "Le Pais aus Englois" ["The country of the English"—Ed.], which refer to the time of St. Louis, and which pour scorn upon the "glais gent" ["frigid people"—Ed.]. The assembly held by the English king at Westminster, his boastful declaration that he will cause his son Edward to be crowned with the crown of France, "sur sa blonde chaviaus" ["on his blond locks"—Ed.], and the English confidence in the favour of "Godelamit" are all ridiculed and treated as fantastically strange. There is still a long way to travel before patriotism comes into being, and yet there rings through the rough stanzas a definite sense of separation from the "glais gent."

Thomas Basin[3] has already covered much of the intervening distance when he says: "In the opinion of many, the English are not human beings and men, but senseless and ferocious beasts, which go about to devour people."

In a second way dawning national consciousness expresses itself. There comes into being a sense of responsibility within the nation for all the different sections of its society. No longer will knights and barons care only for others of their own degree, or perhaps for the lesser folk who owe them personal allegiance. All people in the nation become to some extent mutually responsible for each other's welfare. In this connection it is instructive to compare some of the complaints about the condition of the poor workpeople in France, which abound in fourteenth- and fifteenth-century writings. Buchon gives, bound up with his edition of Mon-

strelet's Chronicles, some verses under the title of "La Complainte du pauvre commun et des pauvres laboureurs de France" (1422),[4] which by no stretch of imagination can be classed as patriotic. The picture of the conditions of peasant life may be distressing enough, but the poor labourer never suggests that the Lords and the clergy ought to pity him because he, like themselves, is French. But when Jean Charlier de Gerson, preaching before Charles VI and the representative nobility, speaks officially in the name of the University of Paris, and puts forward the wrongs of the poor as a common responsibility of the king and his nobles, as he does in the sermon "Vivat Rex" ["Long live the king"—Ed.], some national sentiment at least may fairly be inferred.

To assess accurately the quantity and quality of "national sentiment" in France before the early days of the fifteenth century would demand a minute examination of the events of French history, and men's reactions to them, as recorded in chronicles and journals, as well as a careful study of all works of imagination then extant, both verse and prose, in French and Latin. But a rough estimate may be hazarded after consideration of a few of the more outstanding examples of literary works and historical records.

Dealing first, then with works of imagination already in existence at the beginning of the fifteenth century, the majority of them are innocent of any trace of national feeling. The "Poème par Adalbéron" (*c.* 1010) is an early, but a very fair example. There is much lively satire upon the Church and the lords, but no word of national sentiment. Yet here and there one stumbles upon surprisingly articulate

---

[3] A fifteenth-century chronicler of the reigns of the French kings Charles VII and Louis XI—Ed.

[4] "The complaint of the poor commoner and of the poor laborers of France." The Monstrelet chronicles were also written in the fifteenth-century.—Ed.

and spontaneous expressions of love of country, troublesome exceptions, falsifying any attempts to ennunciate a rule about the absence of national sentiment. There are, for instance, two lines in the "Chronique ascendante des duc de Normandie" ["The continual chronicle of the dukes of Normandie"—Ed.], which run:

Se les Franchiez poeient lor penser achever,
Ja li Roiz d'Engleterre n'arait rien decha mer.[5]

Raynouard, to take another random instance, in his *Troubadours,* gives a poem by Peirols, knight of the Dauphin of Auvergne, composed by him about A.D. 1190. Having fulfilled his vow as a crusader and visited the Holy Places, Peirols is in haste to return to France. He recommends to the mercy of God, Acre and Tyre, Tripoli, Servauts, the Hospital and the Temple: for himself, may Heaven send him prosperous winds:

Qu'a Marcelha m'en vuelh tornar de cors;
Quar s'ieu era de lai mar veramen[6]

About sixty years later (*c.* 1260) came Ruteboeuf's dialogue "La Desputizons dou Croisié et dou Decroisié."[7] In it, "le Decroisié" argues that a man should be able to find God without going to seek him in Palestine, for:

Se dieu est nule part el monde,
Il est en France c'et sens doute.[8]

This whole work foreshadows faintly the conflict which inevitably arose with the stirring of national spirit, between the duty of a knight to the Church universal

[5] "If the French would just concentrate on finishing them/The king of England would have nothing overseas."—Ed.
[6] "So that I may return to Marseilles;/For if I were left behind it would indeed be unfortunate."—Ed.
[7] "The Disputation of the Crossed and the Uncrossed," that is, between a crusader (who had taken the cross) and a noncrusader.—Ed.
[8] "If God is anywhere in the world/He is doubtless in France."—Ed.

and to Christendom, and his proper obedience of his liege lord, the King. The whole problem is set out at length in a Latin dialogue now assigned to Pierre d'Ailly, but at one time attributed to Jean Charlier de Gerson, and therefore included among his collected works. A French and an English solider, meeting by chance in France, discuss the war. The French soldier advances the theory that all Christendom must unite to fight the Infidel, and that Christian knights must never wage war upon each other. But the English knight declares that his first allegiance is to his king and leader. When the Frenchman replies that he ought only to obey in things that are right, the immediate retort is, "I hold that everything is right which the Chief, in consultation with his priests and lords, commands." In vain the French solider argues that no man must give his conscience into another's keeping: the Englishman repeats doggedly that it is not for him to decide; he follows his leader. Thus did Pierre d'Ailly set out the position as he saw it, emphasising the dangers of this new heresy, which, if left unchecked, would disintegrate society—as it most surely did.

Later, the English soldier declares that Normandy at least ought to belong to the English, and that they are within their rights in that matter. "Hold your peace!" cries the Frenchman. "That is not true. You can hold nothing this side of the sea except by tyranny: the sea is and ought to be your boundary."

It is the same cry which had run out in the "Chronique ascendante des ducs de Normandie," and had been repeated in verses called the "Le dit de la rébellion d'Engleterre et de Flandres" (*c.* 1340) ["The Story of the Rebellion of England and Flanders"—Ed.]. The poem, addressed to Philip of Valois, is notable chiefly for one passage, which expresses this sentiment—a sentiment familiar to a later generation, in Jeanne d'Arc's plea of "France for the French." A few lines merit quotation:

"Tu pues bien savoir et congnoistre
Que Englois one Francois n'ama;
. . . .
Et te fais seigneur, droit clamer
De tout ce qui est deca mer,
Soit la mer borne et dessevrance
De l'Engleterre et de la France."[9]

The demand for the expulsion of the English reappears frequently in the works of Eustache Deschamps. The implacable refrain of two of the ballads is well known:

"Paix n'avez ja s'ils ne rendent Calais."[10]

Eustache Deschamps was more deeply concerned for France as a whole than for the triumph of any faction in the State. It is true that he felt no impulse to sacrifice his comfort for the good of France, and that much of his hatred of the English sprang from his private grudge against them for sacking his château near Vertus in 1386. But it was not only the English in France that he hated: his ballads are full of expressions of satisfaction every time that he returns from his many foreign journeys, to "ce doulz pais de France." His appreciation of French beds, French meals, French manners, is set off against his contempt for the customs of other countries: he takes pride, too in the achievements of great men gone, and praises Du Guesclin[11] as "the flower of

heroes and the glory of France." His pity for the downtrodden poor, and his disgust at the mismanagement of the wars and the misgovernment of the ruling classes, provide endless themes for his verses. When Crapelet describes him as "un poète national," or Geruzez speaks of his "patriotisme intelligent," the words are beginning to approach nearer to their modern meaning.

For the sake of brevity these examples must serve. They are sufficient to show that certain elements of patriotism appeared sporadically before the fifteenth century in works of imagination in France.

The first difficulty which must be faced in making any attempt to collect evidence from chronicles is that of determining the date at which the chronicles concerned reached their present form. It is clearly valueless, when trying to assess the state of feeling in France before 1400, to quote extracts from chronicles which, though dealing with the period, and even perhaps based upon contemporary notes, have been edited and adapted by later writers and coloured by their increasingly nationalistic sentiments.

The caution required in this matter can be illustrated by a comparison of the verse and prose chronicles about Bertrand Du Guesclin. In the "Anciens mémoires sur Du Guesclin" ["Old Histories of Du Guesclin"—Ed.] there is an account of the capitulation to the French forces led by Du Guesclin of the inhabitants of La Rochelle: "selon la pente qu'a naturellement chaque nation d'obéir à un prince qui soit de son païs" ["following the natural inclination each nation has to obey a native prince"—Ed.]. But the text of this chronicle, first written in 1387, was modernised at Douai in 1692, by Le Fèvre, and it is this "méchante compilation" ["nasty compilation"—Ed.], as Molinier calls it, which is given by M.

---

[9] "You should know and understand/That no Frenchman loves an Englishman/. . . And to make yourself lord you must claim your right/Over all this side of the sea/Let the sea be the boundary and dividing line between England and France."—Ed.

[10] "There will never be peace until they return Calais."—Ed.

[11] Bertrand du Guesclin (d. 1380) was the French hero of the "middle phase" of the Hundred Years' War.—Ed.

Petitot. Cuvelier's poem, "La vie vaillant de Bertran du Guesclin" ["The Valiant Life of Bertrand du Guesclin"—Ed.], and Guillaume de Saint-André's "Libvre du Bon Jehan, duc de Bretaigne" ["The Book of Good John, Duke of Brittany"—Ed.], which did not pass through the same treatment, contain no such definite statement. To say that, is not to affirm that there was no rudimentary nationalism stirring in France, when "Messire Bertrand" came so near to driving out the English; but it does serve to indicate the danger of placing much stress upon phrases culled from chronicles in their most easily accessible modern editions.

What shall be said, for example, of extracts from the old verse chronicles of Godefroy de Paris? Dated 1303, there is a long complaint about France being given over to servitude, for the French are not listened to, "qui sont nex de la droite mère" ["who are born of a lawful mother," that is, the legitimate or rightful people" —Ed.], but are pushed into the background to make room for favourites of other nationalities, notably the Flemish. When the chronicle was first written, was the point of the complaint that the court favourites were "foreigners"?

The most difficult chronicles to assess fairly in this respect must necessarily be those which were continued, as the years passed, by various writers in some community such as the monks of Saint Denys. Each new chronicler might well recast, or at least edit, much that his predecessor had done. *Les Grandes Chroniques* (Chroniques de Saint Denys) and the Chronicle of Guillaume de Nangis and his continuators are cases in point.

Les Grandes Chroniques, according to Molinier, contain the official explanation of French Royalist policy, for while the sixth book was, he thinks, written by Pierre d'Orgement, the previous volumes were revised by him. It is not safe, then, to state that the views expressed in the first five books, are contemporary ones, but it is permissible to think that it is a more or less accurate picture drawn from life when in the sixth book we get an account of the difficulties created by the Treaty of Bretigny, and the very definite objection of the towns which did not wish to be transferred to a new king. If we can rely in this way on this sixth book, there can be no doubt that these inhabitants had quite a clear sense of being "French," and were firmly opposed to being "made English" by the stroke of an official pen.

The problem seems more difficult in the case of the work of Guillaume de Nangis and his continuators. When, under the date of 1294, we read that the town of Bayonne, surrendering to the English, was guilty of "trahison," can it be counted as evidence of national sentiment at that early date? Or did a later chronicler read his own feeling into the event? We seem to be on somewhat safer ground when, under the date 1327, the continuator explains the working of the Salic Law, and adds that "from another point of view, the people of the kingdom of France could not endure willingly to be put under the submission of the domination of the English."

Bearing in mind this general warning, however, the chronicles do yield some passages of considerable interest. It has often been stated that Jean le Bel and Froissart represent the attitude of mind of the feudal world as yet untroubled by nationalistic fervour, and that they show impartiality between nations, but marked bias between classes, favouring the nobles as against the peoples, in all countries. Jean le Bel is indeed at some pains to explain why he always refers to the King of England as the Noble King Edward, and simply names Philip "King of France":

it is not because he "tenisse bende et parte,"[12] but because Edward followed the advice of his nobles, while Philip was swayed by the counsel of mere clerks.

But the suggestion that until the days of Jean le Bel—that is to say, in the first half of the fourteenth century—the feudal outlook was the only one, must be confronted with extracts from *La Philippide* of Guillaume le Breton, which was almost certainly written before the end of the thirteenth century. In spite of M. Guizot's claim in the introduction to his edition that this work marks the birth of national sentiment, it must be admitted that, read with bias, the *Philippide* impresses the reader first of all as a "feudal" poem. Yet there are lines which it is impossible to explain away: some kind of national spirit was stirring in France in the last quarter of the thirteenth century.

There is, for instance, in the conclusion that urgent appeal to young Prince Louis to restore his boundaries to those fixed "in the days of Pepin," and to see that "no stranger possesses anything in our territory," and it bids him add Aquitaine to his kingdom, so that "the stranger shall no more hold possessions in our kingdom."

A century later Sir John Froissart was writing his vivid descriptions of the glories of feudalism, innocent of any "tache" of patriotism. His impartiality, however, was not viewed with equal enthusiasm in all quarters. There is an interesting entry in the *Journal* of Jean le Fèvre noting that, on 12 December, 1381, letters were sealed with respect to the confiscation of fifty-six "Quayers" which M. Jean Froissart, priest, incumbent of the parish church of Lestines-au-Mont, near Mons, in Haynault, had caused to be written, making mention of

many and divers battles, and deeds of arms performed in the kingdom of France in past times; which fifty-six quayers of romance or chronicles the said M. Jehan Froissart had sent to be illuminated by Guillaume de Bailly, the illuminator, and which the said M. Jehan intended to send to the "King of England, adversary etc."

It becomes increasingly clear that not only did national sentiment fluctuate from time to time in its rudimentary stages, but also that at any one time it might loom comparatively large in the minds of some men, while others were entirely unaware of any national duty and unmoved by any ardent love of France. The outstanding group of such chronicles is the Burgundian. Some historians—as for example the Marquis du Fresne de Beaucourt—express the view that the Burgundian chroniclers deliberately and wickedly shut their eyes to their obvious national obligation, and set themselves to distort history and spread treason. A perusal of the chronicles concerned does not create that impression: it does, however, serve to strengthen the contention that men's outlook was widely diversified in different parts of the land. In these days, when information and opinion are inevitably standardised by daily press and wireless, we have come to expect that all men everywhere shall at least be aware of the same standards, and we incline to the belief that if such standards are disregarded, it must be an intentional, and probably malicious act. We are apt, in consequence, to forget that the chronicler of the Burgundian court in the fourteenth century might think quite differently from the monks of Saint Denys, without deliberately disregarding any known truth or ideal.

The chronicle most freely and frequently criticised as "tainted" is that by

---

[12] "favors any side"; Jean le Bel was a fourteenth-century French chronicler of the Hundred Years' War.—Ed.

Enguerrard de Monstrelet, while the semiofficial *Mémoires de Pierre de Fenin* comes in for similar treatment. That these chroniclers viewed the English and English alliances without repugnance is clear, but that they did so defiantly and against their better knowledge or conscience, seems to remain entirely unproved. To take one example. In Pierre Fenin's chronicle there is a description of the handing over of Rouen by Guy le Bouteiller to King Henry, after he had pretended that he was about to deliver it up to King Charles. The citizens who had plotted with him to give the town to the French king were beheaded, and Pierre Fenin writes that Guy was greatly to be blamed "for this treason"—that is, for allowing his former associates to be beheaded. There is no suggestion that it was "treason" to aid the English: a writer secretly uneasy about, if not ashamed of such a procedure would scarcely choose to speak of "treason" in the same sentence.

Something similar may be said of the three works "Le Livre des Trahisons de France envers la Maison de Bourgogne," "La Geste des Ducs de Bourgogne," and "Le Pastoralet" ["The Book of the Treasons of France against the House of Burgundy," "The Deeds of the Dukes of Burgundy," and "The Pastoral Play"—Ed.]. All three are closely linked together, the first being probably the foundation for the others, and in them all there is a strong party feeling against the Armagnacs,[13] but no trace of national sentiment. In the "Livre des Trahisons" there is an elaborate defence of the murder of Louis of Orléans, and through it all the uneasiness of the writer can be perceived. But the making of alliances with the Eng-

lish passes without comment: there is no suggestion that there might be any need to defend such action. In chapter LVI, for instance, there is an account of how the King gave to the Countess of Artois lands which "Bernard d'Ermaignac" claimed, and he therefore "s'estoit rendu engles" ["went over to the English"—Ed.]. There follows immediately the account of a "marvellous trayson," when the dukes, assembled at Tours, invited the King to escape from his uncles, and put himself in their hands. Many such examples could be given; negotiations with the English are always described openly, as the most natural thing in the world.

In "Le Pastoralet," Panalus (Henry V) is blamed for his greed in desiring to hold all France, but it is never hinted that he should refrain *because he is not French.* Indeed, he is fulfilling the will of "the God Pan" in punishing the wicked quarrellings of the great lords.

Georges Chastellain was also Burgundian in sympathies, and it is his chronicle which contains the statement about the Treaty of Troyes[14] that no better arrangement could possibly have been made for the good of France. Among his other works there is a conversation in verse between England, France and Burgundy, the three being considered as on an equal footing: there is no hint that England and France are "national states," and Burgundy a rebellious dependency. The first suggestion of such feeling comes in the prologue to the first book of the chronicles of the Dukes of Burgundy, where there is a long explanation of Philip's change of front when he "followed his natural bent" and allied himself with Charles VII.

---

[13] A French political faction opposed to the Burgundians.—Ed.

[14] The Treaty of Troyes (1420) provided that Henry V, king of England, would succeed to the French throne on the death of the French king Charles VI.—Ed.

This gradual change of opinion can be traced in several Burgundian chronicles. In the course of the *Journal d'un Bourgeois de Paris,* for example, the bitterly Burgundian attitude at the beginning becomes modified and finally changed into support for the king. This is in part due to the fact that the work is by two hands, and the second writer is in everything more temperate than the first: in part also it is accounted for by the fact that the *Journal* does not seem to have been intended for publication, nor was its writer protected by any important person. It contains the day to day observations of a Parisian. It is, then, instructive to note that towards the close there is a tendency to take for granted some kind of national obligation and sentiment. There is an account of the way in which Pierre Cauchon detained Guillaume de Gamache and his brothers, "without considering that it is the right of all men, of whatsoever state or rank they may be, to repress force by force, and that the natural law which is immutable directs all men to fight for their country."

Historical writings, then, do appear to bear out the suggestions found in works of imagination—namely, that completely articulate patriotism must be sought in vain before the fifteenth century, although certain aspects of national sentiment can be seen here and there, stronger at one time than another, present in one place and absent in the next, but, on the whole, gaining ground and stimulated always by affliction and suffering, though stifled by ease and plenty.

A survey of Castilian literature leads GIFFORD DAVIS (b. 1906), professor of Romance Languages at Duke University, to the conclusion that the idea of nationality was present in the Iberian Peninsula considerably before Spain became a nation. In the chronicles of the later Middle Ages he finds a rising index of protest against the disposition of "national" territory by Castilian monarchs and takes this as evidence that the chroniclers were beginning to think of Castile as a national entity rather than the personal possession of a king.*

Gifford Davis

Castile

Chronologically preceding the modern manifestations of nationalism, that primary devotion to one's state, there must first have developed in the various countries a feeling of unity of background and of future destiny, a realization of common bonds, in other words a sentiment of nationality. The study of the growth of this sentiment in mediaeval Castile is significant for an understanding of modern Spain and of the modern phenomenon of nationalism. Spain was at the opening of the modern period one of the greatest powers in the world. Writers have called it one of the first countries to attain nationhood. This is questionable, for then as now, it was torn by conflicting separatist and centralist movements. But then as now, Castile and the cen-

tral provinces stood more for national unity.

Among the many important indexes to the growth of the sentiment of nationality which the old chronicles and literature offer us is the contemporary judgment of writers concerning the disposition of territory by arbitrary will of their monarchs. Such comment as may be found should help to show whether mediaeval Castilians considered their country as a personal property of the king or as a national possession intrusted to the crown.

Legally the distinction between the king's private property and the *patrimonio real*[1] existed, but in practice the

[1] The "royal inheritance" that is, the crown, the prerogatives of kingship, and the territory of the realm.—Ed.

*From Gifford Davis, "The Incipient Sentiment of Nationality in Mediaeval Castile: the *Patrimonio Real*,"*Speculum,* XII (1937), 351–358. Reprinted by permission of the Mediaeval Academy of America. Footnotes omitted.

kings disposed of the realm much as they saw fit. The criticism which we find centers about two types of royal action: alienation of territory and partition of the realm. In the early years of the Spanish-Christian kingdoms royal marriage, inheritance, or conquest occasionally brought two or more kingdoms under one monarch. That the kings felt they had not added to their original realm but had acquired new realms is suggested not only by their multiple titles but by the frequency with which they separated these kingdoms again among their sons.

The Latin chronicles contemporary with these partitions are impassive. Probably not till the epics of the twelfth century did literature become discursive enough on political and lay subjects to offer evidence. Since those epics which might concern us are extant only in the material preserved in the general chronicles of the late twelfth and thirteenth centuries, we may consider that the chronicles of Lucas de Tuy (the *Tudense*), Rodrigo Jiménez de Rada (the *Toledano*) and Alfonso el Sabio and Sancho el Bravo (the *Crónica General*) offer the first available evidence.

The three chronicles recount without criticism that in 1035 Sancho the Great of Navarre divided his Spanish empire among his sons. They explain Fernando I's partition in 1065 as an attempt to keep peace among his children after his death. They all speak of the strife which followed, attributing it to the fierce jealousy of Gothic blood which ran in the royal veins. But the passage in the *Crónica General,* through its appropriation of legendary, probably epic material, is by far the most striking. Here is quoted the eldest son Sancho's protest against the partition:

. . . et dixo a su padre que lo non podie fazer, ca los godos antiguamientre fizieran su pos-

tura entresi que nunqua fuesse partido el imperio de Espanna, mas que siempre fuesse todo de un sennor, et que por esta razon non lo devie partir nin podie, pues que Dios lo avie ayuntado en el lo mas dello.

["And he said to his father that he could not do it, because the Goths from ancient times said among themselves that the Spanish empire should not be divided. They said, in effect, that the entire country should acknowledge one master and that no one should divide it because God had willed it so."—Ed.]

Sancho in appealing to the Gothic tradition of indivisibility of Spain and to God's will for unity was selfishly adducing a neglected tradition, one which if given later impulsion would be of national import. Doubtless, as the chroniclers stated, the protest rose from fiery ambition, but how better can a leader further his aggrandizement than by appealing to tradition, and how better can a tradition become a national ideal than by serving as a tool to the leader? The passage reveals no overt judgment of the chroniclers, but, as we shall see, the simple inclusion of this appeal for unity had, through the course of later events and of literary imitation, its influence in shaping later thought.

It is tempting but difficult to impute to the chroniclers a critical purpose in their terse recording of these partitions. Yet the comment by Jiménez de Rada (copied by the *Crónica General*) concerning the last division of Castile and Leon by Alfonso VII shows a disapproval which gives weight to the assumption. The king, he says, was acting on the advice of two men seeking to foment violence.

With the final union of Castle and Leon partition of the realms ceased. The theory for this cessation was clearly stated when Alfonso X in his *Siete Partidas* decreed the rule of primogeniture:

. . . los homes sabios et entendudos catando el pro comunal de todos et conosciendo que

esta particion non se podre facer en los regnos
que destroidos no fuenso ... tuvieron por
derecho quel señorio del regno no lo hobiese
sinon el fijo mayor despues da la muerte de
su padre.

["The wise men, aware of the general well-
being, and realizing that this partition would
only fragment the kingdom ... decided that
the right of kingship, by law, devolves upon
one person, the eldest son upon the death of
his father."—Ed.]

But, as we have indicated, partition
was not the only royal act which jeopar-
dized the integrity of the realm. Under
quite different circumstances Portugal
broke away from Leon in the late eleventh and early twelfth centuries. At the
time of Henri de Bourgogne's marriage
to Alfonso VI's illegitimate daughter,
Alfonso gave him in fief the little county
of Portugal, then confined to the basin
of the Duero river south of Galicia. Henri
was successful in his attacks on the Moors
and took their land for himself instead of
rendering it to the crown as he was bound
to do. His son with the aid of the Pope
became the first king of Portugal. The
comment on this in the *Toledano,* quoted
by the *Crónica General,* indicates disapproval:

Mas la bondad del rey don Alfonso et mas la
negligencia, esto es desden de tener oio segund
dize ell arçobispo, et la voluntad que avie el
rey don Alfonso de onrrar a aquel conde don
Henrric como a yerno, se esse conde ganava
tierra et acrescie en su sennorio el rey don Alf-
fonsso nin catava por ello nin fazie y fuerca.

["Because of the kindness of the king and also
because of negligence, and this is something
that one has to beware, said the archbishop,
it was the will of king Alfonso that his son-in-
law Henry be honored if he gains lands and
enlarges the realm. The king would not mind
if this were done by strength."—Ed.]

The harshest word in this criticism is

negligence. Negligence in what respect is
not stated, but obviously it applies to the
administration of the *patrimonio real.*

It is in the *Siete Partidas* of Alfonso X
that one finds the statement concerning
the *patrimonio real,* yet this monarch,
perhaps more than his predecessors, was
guilty of treating the realm as private
property. When in 1258 his daughter
married the king of Portugal he had no
compunction in giving as dowry the eastern Algarbe which he had conquered
from the Moors only the year before.
"Thereafter," says the chronicler, "the
kings of Portugal styled themselves kings
of the Algarbe."

This chronicler repeatedly records the
rebellion of the nobles at Alfonso's continued policy of generosity to foreigners.
When in 1269 Alfonso was taking council
concerning the abolition of the slight
tribute exacted from his grandson, the
king of Portugal, don Nuño González
de Lara declared that, while Alfonso
did much honor to himself in giving his
grandson what was his to grant, he should
not deprive the crown of just tribute:
"Mas, señor, que vos tiredes de la corona
de vuestros reynes el tributo que el rey
de Portugal e su reyno son tenudos de
vos facer, yo nunca, señor, vos le conse-
jaré." ["But, sir, in this you throw away
the crown of your realm as well as the
tribute that the king of Portugal and his
realm are bound to render; that I would
not advise you to do"—Ed.]. Here is a
distinction between personal property of
the king and that of the crown imputed
to one of the most powerful nobles of
Alfonso X's reign. Since harangues were
more than likely to be the work of the
authors and since the chronicle from
which the speech is quoted was not written
until the first half of the following century (fourteenth) it would be bold to
assume that this identical speech was

actually made to Alfonso X. While such a sentiment doubtless existed in his times, it was most surely the feeling of the chronicler who recorded it more than half a century later.

In the last of the fourteenth century a much more significant expression of national feeling was elicited by the startling personal disposition of the realm proposed by Juan I. This monarch, thwarted in his attempts to acquire Portugal, had seen all his diplomatic and military efforts come to naught. The betrothal of his first son to Beatriz, the only child of the king of Portugal, had proved unsatisfactory to the latter. The subsequent betrothal of his second son to the same Beatriz not promising a union of the two kingdoms, he had himself, on becoming a widower, taken her as his second wife. Then not willing to await an heir, as had been agreed, he had at the death of Fernando of Portugal attempted to assert his claims by arms. The result was the rise of the ambitious João d'Aviz and the famous Portuguese victory at Aljubarrota (1385). Unable to relinquish his heart's desire, he presented his council in 1390 with the following plan.

He would renounce the kingdom of Castile and Leon to his minor son Enrique, taking however Seville, Cordoba, the Bishopric of Jaen, all the frontier, the Seigniory of Biscay, and also the income of the *tercias* of the realm of Castile. With these he would call himself king of Portugal and would wear the arms of Portugal.

Pedro López de Ayala, favorite and councilor of Juan I and historian of the reign, records the answers of the council in which he doubtless had his part and in words which are probably his own. The answer is vigorously negative. The first objection is historical, evidencing the influence of national writings. In it is a suggestion of the measured words of the *Toledano* and the *Crónica General* as they describe the results of Fernando I's partition:

[the] corónicas é libros de los fechos de España [showed] quanto mal é quanto daño, é quantas guerras é perdidas han seydo é son en España por las particiones que los Reyes vuestros antecesores ficieron entre sus fijos de los Regnos de Castilla é de Leon.

["The chronicles and books of the history of Spain showed that whatever destruction, wars, and losses there have been in Spain have been the products of the partitions which the kings, your ancestors, made among their children of the kingdoms of Castile and Leon."—Ed.]

After describing the partitions of Fernando I and Alfonso VII and their consequences, the argument continues; God had seen fit to rectify the mistake of these partitions in the union under Fernando III, but the Algarbe, given by Alfonso X, was permanently alienated, and Portugal, lost by Alfonso VI, was not only still separated but was now the cause of the present evils and hostility.

Secondly, the councilors recognized as a practical fact what Juan blindly ignored: the national feeling of the Portuguese. They had already taken arms to prevent the kingdom of Portugal from being merged with the kingdom of Castile. Now with the bad blood that had been aroused they were declaring that they would rather die than obey the king of Castile: "antes llanamente dicen que en ninguna manera vos obedescerán, é que sobre esto morirán é se perderán" ["Frankly, they say that they will never obey you; they will die rather than do this"—Ed.]. How could Juan without the strength of all Castile and Leon hope to effect what he had been unable to do with that strength.

Thirdly they recognized the loyalty to Castile of the provinces which Juan would so ruthlessly sever from it, and declared that in refusing to obey a Portuguese king these provinces would be justified: ". . . ca tienen que son propios de la Corona de Castila, é veyendovos llamar Rey de Portugal é traer armas de Quinas, que son armas de Portogal, é non de Castillos é Leones non vos obedescerán, non paresce que farán en ello sinrazon" ["Because they believe they are naturally a part of the crown of Castile, and calling yourself king of Portugal and wearing the arms of Portugal instead of Castile will avail nothing; it does not seem to us that they act without reason"—Ed.]. Even Biscay, though a land apart, counted itself as under the seigniory and banner of Castile and would not consent to being severed.

Fourthly they recognized the national spirit of Castile itself. An attempt by a king wearing the arms of Portugal to collect taxes in Castile would cause uprising. They pled for the good of the kingdom, fearing the anarchy of a long regency. If division were accomplished, Juan's son would do battle to reintegrate the kingdom. Such a division would weaken the cause of Christendom, and in the eyes of the monarchs of Europe would lower the standing of Castile and Leon as well as Juan's good name.

While actually the word nationality is not used nor the word nation, the whole protest is for the common good of Castile and Leon. Nowhere is there appeal to loyalty to a national state so named, for it is a practical rather than theoretical essay on nationality. The objections to Juan I's plan are based on a recognition of national loyalties and national temper: the Murcians and Sevilians feel they are Castilian; the Biscayans owe their allegiance to the arms and banner of Castile and Leon; the Castilians would not allow their taxes to be collected by those bearing the arms of Portugal. The crown and royal arms appear a symbol and a rallying point of Castilian feeling much as a modern flag has become a symbol of national sentiment.

This crisis, as has been seen, called forth invocation and interpretation of national history. The internal strife and unrest of the following century continued this trend in a significant manner. In the midst of the rebellion of the fifteenth century a nephew of López de Ayala, Fernán Pérez de Guzmán, turned his pen to the praise of the great men of Castilian history. Steeped in the misfortunes as well as the glory of his country's tradition he was charting a course for his own times. With the criticism of the general chroniclers and of his uncle in his mind he wrote in condemnation as well as in praise. He declared that Juan II's great ancestor, Fernando I, was not without fault for, contrary to the customs of the Goths, and to the great detriment and evil of the country, he had divided what God had joined together. One can recognize the very words of the *Crónica General.* Alfonso VII had been equally ill-advised when he divided Leon and Castile. Perez de Guzmán was a moralist; to carry his point he depended not on a fervid appeal but on calm, logical advice:

> Reyes, sed bien avisados
> que partir e diminuir
> es menguar e dividir
> los reynos e principados.
> Son pequeños los estados
> del chico e menudo imperio:
> reyezillos son llamados
> que es gorja e vituperio.
>
> Pueden poco conquistar
> en breve son conquistados
> nunca pueden sojudar
> a siempre son sojudgados.
> Quien fallo grandes venados
> en pequeño monte e breña?

En agua baxa a pequeña
non mueven grandes pescados.[2]

The undoubted Castilian feeling of the poem as a whole imbues this ideal of greatness and strength with a national import.

A similar judgment is that of a Latin chronicler of the following reign, Rodrigo Sancho de Arevalo. Restrained in recounting the earlier partitions, he paused after that of Alfonso VII and drawing on past criticism stated his own theologically tinged ideal of national entity. While partition may be the result of God's will, either avenging or preventing discord, it comes as a result of a people's sin. God's real blessing is in uniting one people under a single ruler. While a king may attempt to prevent dissension by partition of his realm among his sons, one may rather fear that dissension as a result. A kingdom divided is more open to invasion and dissolution, and no realm can survive unsustained by unity.

Thus by the fifteenth century the barely noticeable comments of the general chroniclers have become articles of faith. Then too, the reunions of the two kingdoms, recognized by the early chroniclers without emotion are now commented upon in the light of this faith. Fernán Pérez de Guzmán accounted a great blessing the union of Castile and Leon under Fernando III:

en aqueste se han juntado
los reynos que, por pecados,

por dos vezes apartados
grandes danos han causado.[3]

His contemporary, Alfonso de Cartagena speaking of the same event in his Latin *Anacephalaesis* declared, "And this union obtains today and shall, God directing, obtain forever."

A fitting conclusion to this discussion of Castilian national territory is the enthusiasm shown by Mosén Diego de Valera at the thought of a unified Peninsula. In a letter to Isabel he compares the joining of the crowns of Castile and Aragon to doña Berenguela's successful efforts to join Castile and Leon under Fernando III: 'é bien asy commo la muy excelente reyna Doña Berenguela ayuntó estos reynos departydos, de Castilla é de Leon . . . asy vos, Señora los aveys ayuntado con Aragon é Secilia' ["And so you, the great queen Lady Berenguela, united these separate kingdoms of Castile and Leon . . . in the same way, my lady, that you united those of Aragon and Sicily"—Ed.].

In this there breathes not only the flattery for a queen but a feeling of Castilian destiny. More tenuous than Ayala's practical recognition of a national feeling as a political fact, it is perhaps equally as significant as an index of national feeling.

From the preceding pages it is evident that the general chroniclers of the thirteenth century criticized openly or by implication the partitioning of the realm on the grounds of ensuing civil war. They condemned alienation of territory as kingly negligence. But they made no real national criticism of royal disposition of territory. The early fourteenth-century chronicler of Alfonso X's reign protested his freehandedness in dealing with

---

[2] "Kings be well advised/That to partition and diminish/Is to decrease and divide/Your kingdoms and principalities./The size of states/Is small in a small empire/And they are called kinglets/Which is not very flattering./In this matter they conquer little/But they are quickly conquered/They cannot subjugate/But are always subjugated./Whoever finds large deer in small mountains/In small ponds you do not find large fish."—Ed.

[3] "At this time you have seen united/the kingdoms which through errors/have twice been divded/thus giving great reason for sorrow."—Ed.

the property of the crown. By the second half of the fourteenth century Pedro López de Ayala attributed the danger of civil war following partition not to jealousy, as had the general chroniclers, but to certain loyalties which he did not label but which were clearly national. In support of his belief he drew on traditional criticism first stated in the general chronicles. In this he was followed in the fifteenth century by Pérez de Guzmán and Rodrigo Sancho de Arevalo who frankly condemned the partitions of preceding rulers and who rejoiced as did Alfonso de Cartagena at the final union of Castile and Leon, and as did Mosén Diego de Valera at their union with Aragon. From this increasingly articulate criticism and the more striking feeling of Castilian destiny one may assume that toward the opening of the modern period there existed in Castile a growing national consciousness.

Suggested Additional Readings

The literature of nationalism is too numerous and varied to be included here in its entirety. Fortunately, much of the available material treats only the recent period and thus is not germaine to the more specialized subject of nationalism in the Middle Ages. Nonetheless, the student would do well to familiarize himself with a few modern surveys, for it is in these that he will most often encounter the argument that nationalism is really a subject to be treated only in recent history.

Among the best "standard" treatments of nationalism are the studies of Carleton J. H. Hayes, *The Historical Evolution of Modern Nationalism* (New York, 1931); Hans Kohn, *The Idea of Nationalism: A Study of Its Origins and Background* (New York, 1944); and Boyd C. Shafer, *Nationalism: Myth and Reality* (New York, 1955). Selections from the latter two studies appear in this volume. Perhaps the most significant of all such studies in shaping the general attitude toward nationalism is the influential paperback *Nationalism* (Princeton, N.J., 1955) by Hans Kohn. Boyd C. Shafer has also written for the Service Center for Teachers of History the very readable essay *Nationalism: Interpreters and Interpretations* (Washington, 1959). This work, however, is concerned primarily with definitions of nationalism, and touches upon historical developments rather lightly. Beyond these studies interested students should consult the following bibliographies: Koppel Pinson, *A Bibliographical Introduction to Nationalism* (New York, 1935) and Karl Deutsch, *An Interdisciplinary Bibliography on Nationalism, 1935–1953* (Cambridge, Mass., 1956).

There is no comprehensive study of medieval nationalism. The terms "nationalism," "national sentiment," or "national feeling" occur frequently in the works of medievalists but in most instances the writer assumes the reader accepts the fact that nationalism existed in the Middle Ages and does not attempt to prove the point. Noteworthy exceptions to this are the general essays on the subject by Halvdan Koht, "The Dawn of Nationalism in Europe," *American Historical Review,* LII (1947), 265–280; Jullian Camille, "L'ancienneté de l'idée de la nation," *Revue Politique et Littéraire,* LI (1913), 65–70, 99–103; Marcel Handelsmann, "Le rôle de la nationalité dans l'histoire du Moyen Âge," *Bulletin of the International Committee of Historical Sciences,* II, Part 2 (1929), 235–247; and Karl G. Hugelmann, "Mittelalterliches und Modernes Nationalitäten-Problem," *Zeitschrift für Politik,* XIX (1930), 734–742. There is also a brief treatment of the development of nationalism in the latter Middle Ages in W. T. Waugh, *A History of Europe, 1378–1494* (reprinted with new bibliographies; London, 1960). Most recently the subject has been treated by Johan Huizinga in his "Patriotism and Nationalism in European History," in *Men and Ideas: Essays on History, the Middle Ages, the Renaissance,* translated by James S. Holmes and Hans Van Marle (New York, 1970), pp. 97–155. A portion of this essay is reprinted here, but the whole would be well worth reading as it carries Huizinga's discussion of nationalism into the Renaissance and modern periods. In addition to these later works it is still interesting to read the older studies that postulate the presence of a virulent national feeling in medieval times. Here Oliver Richardson, *The Nationalist Movement in the Reign of Henry III and Its Culmination in the Barons' War* (New York, 1897) is a classic. Also worthwhile reading is the work of the eminent British medievalist Edward A. Freeman, "The Continuity of Eng-

115

lish History," in his *Historical Essays* (London, 1871), pp. 40–52.

Beyond the preceding studies the literature on medieval nationalism becomes rather specialized. Each author approaches the subject from his own interest—law, language, and so on—and attempts to fit his contribution into the general framework of what other medievalists have done. Thus, R. M. Wilson, *Early Middle English Literature* (London, 1939) and R. W. Chambers, *On the Continuity of English Prose* (London, 1932) find evidence of nationalism in their linguistic studies, while G. E. Woodbine, "The Language of English Law," *Speculum*, XVIII (1943), 395–436, and Gaines Post, "Two Notes on Nationalism in the Middle Ages," *Traditio*, XI (1953), 281–320, argue from the legal as well as linguistic point of view. Ernst H. Kantorowicz is primarily concerned with the development of a "nationalist mentality" in "*Pro Patria Mori* in Medieval Political Thought," *American Historical Review*, LVI (1951), 473–484. M. M. Postan briefly treats the importance of economic nationalism in "The Economic and Political Relations of England and the Hanse from 1400 to 1475," in *Studies in English Trade in the Fifteenth Century*, edited by E. Power and M. M. Postan (London, 1933), pp. 91–153.

In addition to the essays published here the role of the medieval church in the development of nationalism is treated in *Nationalism at the Council of Constance, 1414–1418* (Washington, 1927) by George C. Powers and in *Nationality and the Western Church before the Reformation* (London, 1959) by I. P. Shaw. Louise R. Loomis also studies the problem of nationalism and the conciliar movement in her "Nationality at the Council of Constance: an Anglo-French Dispute," *American Historical Review*, XLIV (1939), 508–527. The Loomis study is also valuable for its notation of articles dealing with certain aspects of the "nations" in medieval universities. On the same subject, see the enormously detailed study of Pearl Kibre, *The Nations in the Medieval Universities* (Cambridge, Mass., 1948).

Curiously enough there has not been a great deal written concerning the development of national feeling during the Middle Ages in the various European states. Other than those included in the present volume the most significant are: K. G. Hugelmann, "Die deutsche Nation und der deutsche nationalstaat im Mittelalter," *Historisches Jahrbuch*, LI (1931) 1–29, 445–484; Fritz Kern, *Die Anfänge der französichen Ausdehnungspolitik* (Tübingen, 1910); Gifford Davis. "The Development of a National Theme in Medieval Castilian Literature," *Hispanic Review*, III (1935) 149–160. See also Kemp Malone, "The Rise of English Nationalism," *Journal of the History of Ideas*, I (1940), 504–505, which was written in rejoinder to Hans Kohn, "The Genesis and Character of English Nationalism," *Ibid.*, 69–94.